Beloved and Brain Cancer

Living Each Moment As If It Were Your Last

Dr. Aimee Knauff

BELOVED AND BRAIN CANCER:
Living Each Moment As If It Were Your Last
by Dr. Aimee Knauff
Published by The Lael Agency
Winston Salem, North Carolina
www.LaelAgency.com

No part of this book may be used or reproduced in any form, stored in a retrieval system, or transmitted in any form by any means, electronic, photocopy, mechanical, recording or otherwise without written permission from the author. The only exception is for critical articles or reviews, in which brief excerpts may be used.

Paperback ISBN - 978-1-954433-01-4
Hardback ISBN- 978-1-954433-02-1

Cover Photo: Meridith Mertzlufft

Author's Contact:BelovedandBrainCancer@gmail.com
Website:BelovedandBrainCancer.com

Copyright © 2020 by Dr. Aimee Knauff
All Rights Reserved

First Edition

Printed in the United States of America.

DEDICATION

This is dedicated to my three Beloved children: Sofia, Everest, and Carter. They were the initial reason I started writing.

ENDORSEMENTS

"I have known Aimee since she was a little girl. She was one of those rare people at even a very young age who would light up a room just by walking into it. In a world that is in desperate need of light, she continues to bring light, even through suffering and grief. How is this possible? It is because of her life-long, tenacious belief in the truth of what Brennan Manning once wrote: 'Being the Beloved is our identity, the core of our existence. It is not merely a lofty thought, an inspiring idea, or one name among many. It is the name by which God knows us.' Aimee's full embrace of her identity as God's Beloved has been her lifeline and source of light, as it can be yours."

Rob Morris
Co-founder and CEO of Love146

"I'm not sure if it's her smile, her laughter or her wit that I love about her the most. It's rare these days to find a woman so genuine and smart that she can quickly assess any situation with a profound analysis and a witty joke. With a smile that lights up a room, a heart as pure as gold, and tenacity as deep as the sea, my dear friend Aimee is a true treasure."

Dr. Nina Lewis-Larsson
ND and CEO of Elevated Health and Wellness Clinic in Calgary, Alberta

"To be on the journey with someone when they encounter truth and learn to live in it is a precious gift. I had that opportunity backpacking with Aimee in the mountains of the Wind River Range. We were invited to give a name to our intimate relationship with God in the way we needed to hear it most; for Aimee that name was Beloved. There were many moments of struggle on the trail when I was able to remind her of the Truth - she was Beloved - just as she so often with her bright eyes and contagious smile would remind me of the same Truth. Beloved did not stay in the mountains as a memory but was now the true self in which Aimee was rooted. That Truth has shaped her experiences to not be that of defeat but of faithful living. May Aimee's sharing of her journey be a gift to you and an invitation to give name to the Truth for yourself."

Jamie Jennings Martin (Hephzibah)
Training Coordinator for CCO Experiential Designs

"I met Dr. Aimee Knauff five brain tumors and three kids ago. On paper, she was a student like me, but Aimee turned out to be one of the most important teachers I've had in this world. Short in stature and larger than life, her name became synonymous with the strength to continually get back up and keep going when we were classmates in medical school. Practical, no nonsense, sharp as a tack and knock-you-to-the-floor hilarious, Aimee has basically downloaded her extraordinary life, her 16 year journey with brain cancer and her unique approach to dying into this treasure of a book. Gift this story to your loved ones. There is medicine on every page."

Dr. Annette D'Armata
NMD and Senior Medical Editor for Radio VoxFem
Global Health Minute

"I am humbled and honored to have been Dr. Aimee's neurosurgeon since her early 20s. She is a wonderful person as well as a model patient in spite of having such a difficult diagnosis in such a challenging location of her brain. She has been brave beyond belief in how she has personally prepared for and recovered from her multiple surgeries over the years. She truly exemplifies the highest ideals of humanity by constantly showing by example in both words and actions that she cares about others more than herself. Her humble acceptance of her prognosis, with all the associated disappointments and appropriate grief, but also with gracious and loving insights to share, is truly remarkable."

Dr. Kris A. Smith
MD and Neurosurgeon at Barrow Neurological Institute

"Medical school is challenging. Dr. Aimee was always the friend you could rely on to get around the drivel of it all. She helped keep you focused on what was important; getting through this grueling education program. With her beautiful smile, she has confidence, strength, courage, love, and perseverance that make her friends feel that everything is going to be ok. By allowing me to be a part of her life's journey and struggles, she continues to be an inspiration. God's lessons and gifts are presented to us daily through the people in our lives. The power of Dr. Aimee's journey as a healer and teacher will forever bring comfort and strength for myself and others. I am honored to be even the slightest part of her courageous life story."

Dr. Jean-Luc Le Provost
NMD and CEO of Phoenix Men's Health Center

CONTENTS

FOREWARD
Page 13

CHAPTER ONE
Introduction
Page 17

CHAPTER TWO
Reflections on Death
Page 23

CHAPTER THREE
Reflections on My Childhood
Page 33

CHAPTER FOUR
Reflections on My Service Trips to Haiti
Page 43

CHAPTER FIVE
Reflections on Losing a Sister
Page 55

CHAPTER SIX
Reflections on My Spiritual Journey
Page 71

CHAPTER SEVEN
Reflections on Marriage
Page 81

CHAPTER EIGHT
Reflections on Brain Cancer
Page 101

CHAPTER NINE
Reflections on Why I Went to Medical School
Page 125

CHAPTER TEN
Reflections on Becoming a Mother
Page 139

CHAPTER ELEVEN
Reflections on My Insignificant-Self vs My Beloved-Self
Page 169

CHAPTER TWELVE
Reflections on Where I am Now
Page 183

ACKNOWLEDGEMENTS
Page 199

FOREWORD

I remember the TV Ad for a product promising to end messes quickly and cleanly so we can enjoy the moments we have to live. I understand the ad's intention and yet, after reading Aimee's reflections, it seems to me that, if I cannot find present-moment joy in the mess of things, I would probably not find joy in their clean-up or in any other moment of my life.

Aimee invites us to present-moment joy in her real life reflections that are so human, sometimes painful, funny, graphic, earthy, but all the same, believable and loving. Her gratitude for life and her joy in living, comforts, confirms and challenges me to live gratefully and joyfully. I trust she will move you to trust your own life more deeply, to do the work of love with joy.

Aimee literally "re-collects" herself, continually remembers and returns, retrieving the emotional pain and personal behaviors each of us might cringe at remembering, let alone put in writing for others to see. Aimee's "review of life" springs from a powerful and personal spirit, one can even say the Holy Spirit, breathing in her and through her, precisely as her. Strengthening her to grow more deeply human, to understand more deeply her bond with all beings, and to return again and again to encourage others to choose life.

Reading into the past, sometimes painful and unfinished, and resolving into the fullness of healing and forgiveness can be a lesson for all of us. Remembering how easily we can forget our Beloved-self, yet each of us can also come to a peaceful and present moment awareness. Remember how you are at one and the same time wounded and healer; able to turn your own tears of isolated self-pity into tears that cleanse and soften your heart. Set free powerful energy for kindness and compassion for yourself, every person in your life and for all life everywhere.

I found myself living and breathing Aimee's life experiences. I have been so privileged to have a bit of a front seat for certain moments of Aimee and Adam's lives, I know them both in some intimate ways: her children, her family, Adam's family. I know them and I love them, even more as a take in this delightful, serious, hilarious at times, mind and heart forming narrative.

In her poem NEVER AGAIN, Aimee, at fourteen years of age, ponders the life of her sister Candi who died so early in her life:

Never to see her again
Never to come home again
Never to breathe with life again.

Not today Aimee, Beloved with brain cancer, Beloved of Adam, Sofia Faye, Everest and Carter George. Your life is so precious, for your mom and dad, for Adam's mom and dad, your brother, your extended family, your health care colleagues and caregivers, and your friends, including this one here.

There is no time to lose; time only for this breath now and not one moment later, only this love now and not one moment later, and, yes, even the time for the miracle of death but not one moment sooner!

George Strohmeyer
Gannon University
Vice President for Mission and Ministry
and University Chaplain, Retired

CHAPTER ONE

Introduction

My name, Aimee, means *Beloved* in French. From a very early age, I knew that unconditional love was the answer to everything, but what does it really mean to be the Beloved? My journey to discover more about this truth has not been an easy one. Over the course of my life I have found love, but I have also experienced many heartaches and much suffering along the way. In addition, when I did discover the truest gift of unconditional love, it came to me in very unexpected ways.

Looking back over my life, it seems that from a young

age my first mission was to find someone who could love me for all that I am. I set out to find unconditional love in every possible avenue, and I did find love. I found it in my husband, my children, my family and friends, my church, and my community. However, I frequently felt disappointed with love that was based on me being or doing or dressing or thinking in a certain way – in other words, with conditions. I have to admit, though, that I also love others conditionally, even when that's not my intention. Trust me, I'm far from perfect!

It was only through struggling with the shock, fear, and pain of a diagnosis of brain cancer that I was able to experience God's love firsthand. In these instances, I discovered that there is only one source of the unconditional love I was so desperately seeking. I learned firsthand that the God who created me, who knew every cell in my body before I was even born (even the stem cells that would later become brain cancer), has always considered me to be His Beloved.

God has guided my path since birth, and I am humbled to look back and see His hand at work in my life, day by day and year by year. We all have doubts, questions, and struggles, but there is something radical about hope.

God has given me the ears to hear His whispering voice amidst the craziness of life. I decided to really live each moment that I have been given, and in doing so, I hope that I have been able to live the kind of life that God has dreamed for me. I say this because God is the only reason that I am still alive, so I believe that He still has work for me to do. He still has love for me to give.

This excerpt from an early journal reads as if my naïve 19-year-old self is offering my battered 40-year-old self some encouragement to keep writing:

> I will write and write and write until my soul is purged of its eternal struggle. Until I no longer know the heat of passion, the cold of loneliness, the depths of pain, the universe of dreams. I will write until the search is over. Until my longing is washed away by contentment and peace. Until my heart is satisfied. I will write until my last words have been said. Until my soul is empty. Until I can no longer feel or think. Until that day comes, I will write.

Throughout this book I will also include a few of my poems, most written in my youth, that I feel continue to be as powerful and relevant today as they were when I wrote them.

Now, I'll warn you up front: I am Catholic, and I realize that my story gets pretty spiritual at times. I hope for those of you who don't appreciate religion, or organized religion, that you will still continue reading. Feel free to put what I'm saying into a word or phrase you are more comfortable with (Allah, a Higher Power, the Universe, Yahweh, the

Buddha, Great Spirit, the Divine, Mother Earth, etc.), but please don't stop reading. Each chapter shares different lessons I've learned in my life that I think apply to all people, not just those with cancer or who are near the end of life.

Something else to know up front: in my writing, I frequently refer to God using masculine pronouns. However, I also believe that God transcends gender. God is the Intelligent Designer who set off the Big Bang: the creator of the evolutionary process. The Great Spirit is truly beyond the forms of language that we limited human beings have developed. In trying to describe a Being who exists outside of time and space, we have to make do the best we can. So I am sorry if the masculine words I use make you uncomfortable. To be honest, they make me uncomfortable too, but then so would the use of female or plural pronouns. Because Jesus was a man and used masculine pronouns to describe God, I have also decided to refer to God in that way. Until our language catches up with the mystery of the Divine, choosing certain pronouns has to be good enough. To the best of my ability, that is what I have done here.

As mentioned above, I believe this book can help every reader who picks it up. Each one of us is struggling with something in life, whether it's cancer or a chronic illness (including Covid-19), feeling depressed or anxious, being a caregiver, being laid off or furloughed, grieving a

Introduction

loved one, going through divorce, loving someone who is struggling with addiction, or dealing with whatever else life has handed you. At one point or another, each of us asks the question "Why?" about life. As I share my story, I hope that some of the lessons I've learned can apply to your daily struggle as well, as you learn to live each moment as if it were your last.

Peace be with you.

CHAPTER TWO

Reflections on Death

"But do not ignore this one fact, Beloved, that with the Lord one day is like a thousand years and a thousand years like one day."
2 Peter 3:8

Looking at this chapter's title, you're probably asking yourself: "Why did she start with a chapter about death when she said this book was about life?" Well, here's why.

When I start a new book, I skip to the end and read the last couple of pages to see how the story turns out. Because I think most people do that too, I am putting the last chapter first, so that way, I can save you some page flipping.

Now, I'm sure that most people reading this book weren't really looking for the first chapter to be about death. However, I feel like this is an important place to start because it is something that each one of us will experience at some point.

Death has always been a conversation in my family. I was diagnosed with brain cancer right before my wedding, which made my husband Adam and I consider death long before most people do. My kids know that I probably won't be around as long as their friend's moms are—that I likely won't be here to see them graduate high school or college, to be proud of who they become, to celebrate their weddings or the birth of their babies, or to be a proud grandma as their kids grow up.

As a physician myself, I want to be honest with my kids about the process of death. I prefer opening up the conversation now so they know that I am here whenever they have questions or something they want to discuss. I also want to be an example for them on how to live vibrantly, all the way up to death and beyond. This, though, is a lesson that has taken me almost 40 years to learn.

Father Mike Schmitz with Ascension Presents has quite a few videos on YouTube that explain Catholic theology in a very down-to-earth way. He has one called "Why We Say *Memento Mori*" that I found particularly interesting.

Memento Mori is Latin for "Remember your death." This phrase is how early Christians would greet each other; by reminding the other person that we need to constantly be aware of our own death, living each day in preparation for the day that we enter into the presence of God.

Father Mike says that this phrase is especially powerful and profound because so few of us actually remember and reflect on our own deaths, and even fewer of us actually prepare for this event. For each of us, though, one day will eventually be our last.

"But if I haven't done anything to prepare for that day, what do I think is going to happen when I'm standing before God and He asks me to make an accounting for my life?", Father Mike asks the listener. "To remember your death is something so profound and absolutely necessary for the Christian."

However, the term *Memento Mori* doesn't just reference the future: it also refers to the past. As Father Mike puts it in this video: "Remember you have died. What does St. Paul say? He says, 'I have been crucified with Christ. So the life I live now is no longer mine.' You've been purchased at a price." It is important to remember that we have already died in Christ, particularly because there is so much anxiety and fear in our world right now.

"What if you already died?" Father Mike also asks. "Dead men fear nothing. Dead men are anxious about nothing. Imagine that freedom. Imagine the freedom of actually remembering your death on a regular basis. Waking up and saying, 'I've died already. Lord, what do you need from me today? Lord, I've died already. There is nothing I need to be afraid of. There is nothing I need to be anxious about. There is nothing I need to worry about.' Why? Because I've already died. So few of us look to the future with joy and with hope... He's the one I'm living for. Because of that, you can live with joy right now in anticipation of the joy you'll step into the moment you die with God's grace."

Even before I saw this video and other from Father Mike's series, I already believed that death is going home. On this side of the veil, everything that happens in your life might seem random, unconnected. However, when you die, then you turn the page of time and are finally able to see through the veil. You will see how your one thread spreads through so many others, all coming together in various ways to make a beautiful tapestry that God has created spanning from the beginning of time until the end.

I also think that you're still here on earth in spirit after death. While the people you love can't see you, I do believe that you can see them. My middle son recently asked, "How will I speak to you? How will we talk when you're gone?" I told him: "You just have to share what you want to say and be quiet enough to hear me respond. Trust me, I'm sure I'll answer, but it might get lost in the craziness of life unless you learn to be quiet. Your silence will enclose my words as in a vase. Emptiness shelters sacred space."

My ancestors are still alive in me, seeing my children and my life because they are where I am. They are in every cell in my body. In turn, I will always be with my children, grandchildren, and beyond. In 2 Peter 3:8, God says that a day is like a thousand years, and a thousand years are like a day. This leads me to believe that because time is relative for God, Heaven is the eternal now. We will all get to Heaven at the same time, even though on earth it might have been many years since your loved one passed. When you're in Heaven and start thinking about your spouse, your child, your grandparent, or your friend, you'll turn around and there they'll be.

There is a medical television show called *New Amsterdam* that had an episode featuring a girl who was dying from the return of her cancer. She asked Dr. Sharpe, played by Freema Agyeman, what death would be like. Dr. Sharpe's response really moved me.

She tells the girl, "I think that it's like this."

She sets a chair with her parents behind her and has the girl come and sit down. The doctor then says, "So, when it happens, you won't be able to see your Mom and Dad, and they won't be able to see you. But they will always be there."

"And I'll always be here?" the girl asks.

"Yes, you'll never stop thinking of each other; you'll never stop talking to each other. You'll just be on a different side of the room," replies Dr. Sharpe.

The girl looks up and asks "Mommy? Can you hear me?"

Her mom, with tears in her eyes, answers, "Yes, Babydoll."

"We can hear you little one," her dad chimes in.

"I can hear you too!" the girl says, smiling.

This episode does a good job describing my own understanding of death too. I think that once you have crossed over the veil, which you and I can't see during our earthly lifetimes, we'll still be here in spirit. Really, I am so fortunate to have the chance for a long, slow goodbye to everyone and everything that I love. I actually hope my funeral is a party: a chance for people to come and eat, dance, tell jokes and stories about me. I hope that they laugh until their sides hurt the next day, and that they celebrate that I no longer have the disease I have struggled with for most of my adult life.

Trust me, I will be full of joy: delighting in your laughter from a place where I am truly healed. Then the miracle we have prayed for has happened! I will be absolutely healed, inside and out.

For those to whom this all just sounds too good to be true, there is something for you here too. Think about it this way: even if Heaven is a farce and we just cease to exist—in that case, after death you will no longer struggle with the pain you are currently experiencing. Your life is done, and you are finally set free. You can truly Rest In Peace.

For me, though, I have chosen to give my suffering and struggles to God, and He in turn has transformed me. The fleeting gifts that I have on earth are already fading away: my memory, my analytical brain, my ability to speak and write, my joy in being surrounded by lots of people, my ability to find words. However, I believe that all these things – and more – will be restored in Heaven by a God who is perfect love. He gifts us with justice that we don't deserve and mercy we cannot earn. My Beloved-self will enter Heaven, but what is of this world, I will shed with joy at the gates. Then I will see God in all His glory, and I will sit in awe at His feet.

Jesus still has His crucifixion wounds in Heaven, wounds that His followers know Him by. The holes in His hands, His feet, and His side are evidence of His love for His Father and all of us. I think our personal scars do not go away in Heaven either. There all of the changes to my brain, the ones that scare most doctors who look at my MRI scans, will be outlined in gold, shining for all to see.

I don't think our Heavenly selves will look the same as on earth. However, I will recognize you in your resurrected self, just as you will recognize me. The perfect self can only be seen when the veil of Heaven is parted: this is the you that is perfected and glorified in Heaven. I have a hard time even fathoming that right now while I am still confined to an imperfect self. Yet through all the sadness and pain, I still look forward to that day.

No matter how long you spend on this earth, when we get to Heaven we will be together as if no time has passed. This is the meaning of Revelation 21:4; that, when we are in His presence, we will no longer suffer the longing and loss that we experience here on earth. We will live with true joy and perfect peace because we will be in the presence of God, experiencing all the radiance of who He is. As much as I love and cherish every minute of my life here on earth, I also long for my Heavenly home.

death comes upon us
day
by
day
by
day
sometimes weighing heavy
pressing hard on our shoulders
pressing us into the ground
into the grave
sometimes death is painless
as a stealthy robber in the night
stealing from us
while we remain unaware
but death is always upon us
numbering every breath
counting down
until the last

(20 years old)

CHAPTER THREE

Reflections on My Childhood

"Beloved, if God so loved us, we must also love one another."
1 John 4:11

I am the firstborn of three children. On a snowy day in January, my parents welcomed me into the world. My sister, Candi, was born in October of the next year, when I was just 22 months old. Rob, my brother, then joined our family four years later.

My mom is also a firstborn child; she is the oldest in a family of five children, all born one after the other. She went from pushing a pretend stroller in her toddler years to pushing a real stroller by the age of five. Even though she had to help her mother take care of her younger siblings, my mom couldn't wait to be a mother to her own babies.

Mom planned on having a natural birth, but she was in a lot of pain as my birth neared. The doctor encouraged her to try an epidural; a brand-new procedure that wouldn't affect the baby, they told her, just block the delivery pain. The anesthesiologist gave her the epidural lying down, which blocked just the uterus and did not travel down to the pain coming from the cervix. Believing they had given her the maximum dosage and there was no way she could still feel pain, they went ahead with the delivery. When she screamed and practically leapt off the table with the episiotomy, they realized she wasn't as numb as they had thought. The anesthesiologist quickly put her under just as I was born, allowing my dad to be the first one to hold me.

At the time they didn't have ultrasounds, so my parents didn't know my sex before my birth. My dad was really hoping for a boy to pass on our last name; however, I stole his heart as soon as he held me. To this day, he still calls me "the apple of his eye."

When my mom woke up from her sedative haze, she was overwhelmed with joy and love to finally have a precious baby of her own. Once she picked me up in the delivery room, she practically never put me down again. People say I never cried as a baby: maybe that's why? She also decided to breastfeed me and make homemade baby food, which were not common practices at the time.

22 months later, my sister came along, although they didn't know her sex either until she was born. When they saw that she was a girl, they named her Candice, or Candi for short. This time, delivery was very difficult for Mom. Her obstetrician had difficulty pulling Candi out with forceps around her enlarged head. My dad looked on with nauseous fear as the doctor repeated over and over "I can't get her!" Candi was also purple at birth and took a long time to cry. With a very big, misshapen head, she was not at all attractive to look at. My dad was traumatized by the whole ordeal, and once she was out and breathing, he left the delivery room to take a breath and collect himself. "A child only a mother could love," my mom thought when she first saw Candi. She felt a responsibility to love her daughter even more because she feared no one else would.

The name "Candice" means pure, innocent, shining; all perfectly describe who my sister was, and why so many people fell in love with her. She brought joy and laughter to everyone she met, shattering my mother's initial fear that no one would love her. Candi was an inspiration to all who knew her.

Candi was also born with a condition called hydrocephalus. This condition happens when your body makes extra cerebrospinal fluid that surrounds your brain. For Candi, it put so much pressure on her head that it actually got bigger, and you could see the whites above her eyes because the fluid was pushing them down. Her illness and surgeries were very difficult for me, but we'll talk more about that in a later chapter.

My brother Rob was born when I was five years old. When he first came home, he slept in a cradle on the first floor, and I remember just sitting there and staring lovingly at him. My dad was really proud to finally have a son, and my mom loved having three children of her very own to love and care for.

Candi's illness caused her to have some developmental delays. She seemed to accept that she would never catch up to me, but when Rob came along, he was a big motivation for her. There was no way her little brother could learn things before she did! When he could tie his shoes, she wanted to learn how to tie her shoes also. When he learned to ride a bike, she wanted to ride a bike too. Because of this, Candi and Rob had a very close relationship.

I, on the other hand, felt like I was miles ahead of both Candi and Rob. As a firstborn child, it was like I came out of the womb with a drive to succeed beyond my years. I wanted to achieve perfection in everything I did, sometimes to a fault. When I came home with an A grade on a test, I cried because it wasn't an A+. I always felt that I could relate better to adults than the other kids my age, a feeling that continues even to this day. From a very young age, I knew that I had gifts only I can offer to make a mark on the world. In fact, my second-grade teacher once said that I was so gifted in language arts that she knew I would someday be led to write a book. I was so inspired by her foresight 32 years ago, and the many people throughout my life who said the same thing, that now writing is exactly what I am doing!

During my childhood, my dad's job was always stressful. On a daily basis, he would come home and expect us to be there waiting to greet him and then "talk loudly" at my mom, who was busy making dinner, about how frustrating his workday was. If we were not behaving perfectly or if we interrupted him to ask a question, he would go off at us instead. We quickly learned to just stay away when he got home.

I also have to admit that I was a very stressed and nervous child. I think that it was related to my sister being in the hospital so often – between her needs, and my sick aunt and her baby who moved in with us soon afterward, we were constantly at a different doctor's office for something. At the time, I was just trying to hold myself together. I started biting my nails at a young age, as well as suffering stomach aches when things got overwhelming. I know now that both of these are signs of a child just trying to deal with stress as best they can. I remember frequently going to the nurse's office because my stomach hurt.

I also started showing a change in my emotions. When I felt angry, I took it out on Candi and Rob. Sometimes

I did things I am now embarrassed to admit, and I have since apologized over and over to Rob for my behavior. I'm lucky that he has always loved me and didn't pay me back for what I put him through when he grew bigger than me—a warning my mom often gave me while growing up.

For instance, I remember vividly a time when Rob was maybe two years old, definitely still in his car seat, and I gave him a Tic Tac breath mint. He took it from me and immediately put it in his nose! We had to go to the ER to have it removed, and I'm sure my parents were not at all happy with me...

Another time, in 1987, we moved into a new house my dad had built. My mom sent the three of us out to play in the backyard, something she often did when we were too active inside. The kitchen slider opened out to steps that didn't have riser boards in place, so you could sit under the steps and see out. This is where my brother was playing one time, soon after we moved in. He wouldn't do what I told him to, so I warned him, "If you won't do what I said, I'm going to pour my lemonade on you." He was like, "Yeah right, you're not going to do that," and continued doing whatever it was that upset me. So, having to stick with my threat, I poured lemonade all over his head and face. He then ran inside and got me in trouble, even though it had made sense to me – I only poured the lemonade to punish him for not doing whatever I said! Looking back, this is something I can completely see my own kids doing, and me reacting in the same way my mom did. Oh to be a child again!

Another time, I remember sitting in the family room sewing something. Rob came in and must have been doing something that got on my nerves. I don't know what possessed me, but when he came over to me, I took an embroidery needle (which is bigger than a regular sewing needle and has a sharper tip) and I stabbed him in his behind! Other times, knowing Rob would be watching TV in the family room, I would run down the stairs and scream at him or smack him on the head. It's so embarrassing to remember these incidents; I'm shaking my head as I write this.

Of course, all of this took place while Dad was at work, which perhaps perpetuated my negative behavior. When Rob was in high school and super tall (he is 6'3" and I'm only 4'11"!), it had been years since the last time I did anything, yet he still would still wince when I walked by.

For many years I had no time or space for my siblings. This all changed when my sister Candi died. Losing her brought on a great deal of guilt for how I had treated them both. I think it was really hard for Rob because they were always together, and I felt bad for being so short-tempered with him.

When I moved away for college, I started to really miss both of them and was much kinder to my brother. When I learned that my husband's older sister was nice to him, it made me feel even worse. She was always there: feeding Adam and playing with him and tutoring him. He was very lucky to grow up with someone to look up to.

Even now, I still apologize to Rob because I feel so terrible about how I was with him while he was growing up. Rob now has an amazing wife and two kids who get along fantastically. They must be doing something right—maybe he encourages his kids not to act the way I used to!

This experience came with its life lessons too, even if I didn't understand them in the moment. Every time I would hit my siblings or poke them or any of the other terrible things I did, my mom would always say, "You'd better make it right with them." She always told us to be kind to one another because in the future you'll want to be friends with your siblings. In her own words: "They are the only people who've been in your life from the beginning." Man, how true those words have proven to me now. I truly value my friendship with my brother! He's the only one that has been through it all, which helps to chase away the loneliness I feel at times.

I constantly share this truth with my own children. They regularly gang up, two against one, and who is getting picked on by whom changes throughout the day. I never know who is getting along or not, because the way it so often goes, someone's crying one minute and happy the next. I hear my mom's voice in my head every time I tell them, "Be kind to one another. In the future you will want to be friends with each other."

Looking at them through the lens of everything I know now, I can see that Sofia has inherited a lot of my personality traits, including my not-so-nice big sister trait. (To be honest, all of my children have a tinge of that one, though!) They can all be really kind to each other or pretty mean. And, in a strange kind of paradox, I've realized that what I'm saying sounds like craziness to them now in the same way that it did to me when I was their age.

I realize too that growing up is tough, and it's hard to put it all into perspective before actually growing up yourself. Hopefully, though, my children will grow to see that I was speaking truths to them—truths that I hope they will also pass down to their own children in turn.

You have been
The sweet little baby
I would gently hold,
The active child
Who frustrated me,
The questioning teenager
Looking to the future,
The young adult
Pursuing your dreams,
The mature adult
Married with children,
The seasoned adult
Hoping to leave good memories,
Everything you do
An expression of our ancestors,
All making me thankful
To have you as a sibling
And a friend.

(40 years old)

CHAPTER FOUR

Reflections on My Service Trips to Haiti

"Listen, my Beloved brothers [and sisters]. Did not God choose those who are poor in the world to be rich in faith and heirs of the kingdom that was promised to those who love him?"
James 2:5

My parents often remind me of the time we went on vacation over Christmas break, when I was 11, just about to turn 12. We took the train to New York City. I had been given some money that year, and of course I brought all of it to spend in the "Big Apple." However, as we were walking around the city, we came across a homeless man begging. I had a really strong desire to help him, so I decided to give him all of my Christmas money. Even then at that young age, I knew he needed it far more than I did. In the time since, I have seen that there are so many people around the world, including in our own towns and neighborhoods, who are poor and disadvantaged. I didn't know why at the time, but now I see that my awareness and compassion for the needy is a gift.

When I was in the first grade, several missionaries came and spoke to my church. They said that they had a small mission in Haiti and asked if a team from our congregation would come down and help them build a church. My dad felt the call and decided to go. When we took him to the airport, I remember sitting on the floor sobbing after he left. Not because I would miss him, like people thought, but because I wanted to go with him.

From that day on, when people asked me what I wanted to be when I grew up, I always replied, "A missionary in Haiti," often to a completely shocked adult. I suspect they would silently wonder things like: *How did she know what a missionary was? And how did she know where Haiti was?* I know I would, if I heard a child that young telling me the same thing! That's another bit of perspective I've gained since growing up myself.

My family kept in touch with the mission, though, supporting several children there and receiving regular newsletters that I would read with great interest. I learned that Haiti is one of the most poverty-stricken countries in the world, and even from a very young age, I have always had a heart for the poor. When I was 12, the age my daughter is right now, the mission's newsletter advertised a week over summer break for teens to come down and experience mission work firsthand. I was sold. I knew this was where God wanted me to be, and surprisingly, my parents agreed.

Shortly thereafter, I came across a passage in Jeremiah that further encouraged me to go. Chapter 1, verses 5-7, reads: "Before I formed you in the womb I knew you, before you were born I dedicated you, a prophet to the nations I appointed you. 'Ah, Lord God!' I said, 'I do not know how to speak. I am too young!' But the Lord answered me, Do not say, 'I am too young.' To whomever I send you, you shall go; whatever I command you, you shall speak." To me, these spoke to the situation at hand exactly, solidifying my belief that God wanted me to go on this mission.

My parents made a deal with me: if I could save enough money to cover the mission fee, they would pay for the airline ticket. I'm sure they thought I would never be able to do it, as money had always burned a hole in my pocket. What they didn't reckon with, though, is that going to Haiti was something I really wanted and so, several months later, I had saved up enough from babysitting and other odd jobs. Although I'm sure my parents were floored that

I'd managed it, they kept up their end of the bargain and bought me the plane ticket.

When they opened the plane door in Port-au-Prince, the capital city of Haiti, it was so hot that it felt like someone opened an oven door. We stood in really long lines, sweating profusely as they carefully checked each passport. After I cleared customs, I walked into this huge room that had all of our luggage thrown into a big pile. I finally found my bags, but instead of putting them through an x-ray machine, there were tables where the employees actually looked through each bag. Again the lines were long and I used my ticket to fan myself, wondering for just a moment if this trip was really a good idea.

After I got my bags back, I walked outside, shoving my way through a crowd of Haitians, all talking and yelling in Creole. While I was looking for the mission's truck, I had to ward off Haitian men with airport badges offering to carry my bags or drive me where I needed to go. I finally found the men from the mission, and we loaded up and started the two-hour journey from Port-au-Prince to the mission in Léogâne.

I was shocked by the devastating poverty of the capital city. There were so many people with ripped shirts and unmatching shorts or skirts, walking past brightly painted concrete shops all selling the same things. Huts ranging from concrete to dirt stood behind the shops, as far as I could see. Burning garbage lined the streets. We swerved around Haitian women crossing the street with full baskets balanced on their heads. Little kids knocking on the truck window spoke the only English they knew: "*Blanc, blanc* [which I later learned means "white person"], give me one dollar?"

The dirt road became bumpier as we neared the mission. We passed many villages, with rows of dirt huts on one side of us and a river on the other. The water became dirtier and dirtier as we got closer to the ocean. We'd drive by people bathing in it, then soon afterwards, a pig relaxing in the same water, and then just a little further, people filling jugs to use at their huts while kids splashed around and played. All in the same filthy water! The mission in Léogâne was actually ocean-side, and when you looked up and down the coast, you could see the squalid river water staining the blue ocean water brown.

All of this broke my heart in a way I had never experienced before. And yet, during the week that followed, I was amazed at how happy the Haitian children were. In every village we visited, whether it was to pass out food and clothes, visit a school, go to the prison, or attend a church service, it was always the children who stole my heart. "*Tiblanc!*" they would lovingly call me, which I learned meant "little white lady." It was then that I knew I would forever leave a piece of my heart in Haiti.

I went back the following summer, at age 13, with my two best friends. I also returned again in October with my parents, though this time, to a very restless country that was going through a violent coup d'état to overthrow the elected President, Jean-Bertrand Aristide. On our way to the airport we passed several recently killed bodies lying in the street and learned that people were afraid to speak out because the military would *Koupe tet boule kay!*, meaning, *Chop off your head and burn your house down!* Just days after we left the country on this third trip, the U.S. stopped flights into and out of Haiti altogether, along with stopping assistance to the Haitian government, imposing trade embargoes, and imposing sanctions targeted at the military leadership blocking Aristide's return.

In March of 1995, though, Aristede returned to power and said Haiti was a "secure and stable environment." Flights to the country resumed, and I visited again that summer at the age of 15, staying for a month this time. It was during this trip that I met Ticam, a young Haitian woman and mother to a beautiful little boy named Garan, meaning *guardian* in French. Ticam spoke English, so I could communicate with her from the beginning of my time there. She was a translator for the mission, and although she taught me Creole, she taught me so much more than just the language. In addition, Ticam helped me see the true meaning behind their lives.

One time, Ticam wanted to go to the market, and the missionaries said I could go with her. She took all the money she had saved in order to buy ingredients for that evening's meal. We went in a TapTap, a brightly-painted pickup truck that served as a taxi of sorts in Haiti (the name literally means "quick, quick"). In a TapTap, there are benches in the back and a roof overhead. Looking back, I now realize that Ticam also had to have enough money to pay for both our ride to the market and back home.

Ticam and I got on first, and I thought it would fit maybe six or eight more people. Oh, no! By the time we reached our destination, I was completely squashed between a guy with a goat and an entire family of six. Across from me, Ticam was sitting next to a woman with baskets stacked up on her head. There was also a man with a stack of little chairs, another woman holding a crying baby in one hand and a young boy in the other, and several other people. Once the TapTap was filled to the brim with paying riders, it followed a fixed route until you were ready to get off. When you wanted it to stop, you just tapped on the side of the vehicle and the driver would stop and let you off.

We got to the open market safely that day, which in my opinion was a small miracle. I immediately noticed that there were so many different vendors. We passed tables of vegetables, fruit, toothpaste and other toiletries, various candies, flip-flops made from old tires, and little chairs (the same as the ones the guy on the TapTap carried). Some tables sold lots of different things, while others sold only one. When we passed the first meat vendor, I saw that the meat at first appeared brown, like it was cooked.

However, when you walked by or stopped to look, hordes of flies would erupt from the raw flesh. The sight made my stomach turn.

Ticam bought all of the ingredients she needed, including fly-riddled beef from one of the vendors, and we returned to her home village on a different TapTap.

I then watched Ticam make dinner outside over a small fire. She used lime and hot water to clean the beef, and then she mixed the vegetables, spices, and meat in a beat-up pot. The Haitian beef stew, or *bouyon bef* as she called it, had the most wonderful smell. *Bagay sa ap ba-ou fos!* she told me, *This stuff will give you strength!*

After Ticam fed Garan and I, and then ate some herself, there was a good amount left over. I knew she had spent everything on the meal and the travel, so I was excited that she would have enough to feed herself and her son for several days.

"No," Ticam said when I told her this. "My neighbor has no money for food and they have not eaten today. The children have not eaten. I am taking the rest of the stew to them. God will take care of me and my son tomorrow."

It was like the world was turned on its axis as my materialistic mind was blown open. With her words, Ticam taught me what Jesus really meant when he gave his followers the two main commandments in Luke 10:27, which states "You shall love the Lord, your God, with all your heart, with all your being, with all your strength and with all your mind." And again in Matthew 22:39, where He says: "The second one is like it: You shall love your neighbor as yourself."

Haitians truly love one another. One would think Haitians would horde the few belongings that they have, but during my time there I saw the opposite to be true: they give what little they have, trusting that God will take care of tomorrow. Ticam did not hope God would take care of her or wonder where her next meal was coming from. She knew that God would provide, and so she became the means by which God would provide for her neighbors. The people of Haiti truly trust and care about each other, and this is why they are so happy. They would give the shirts off their backs, which literally may be their only clothing, to help another. Watching how they lived helped me understand that true service with no words is more powerful than passionate words with no service.

In *Going Home: Jesus and Buddha as Brothers*, Thích Nhat Hanh encourages us to stay in the present moment by practice. In the Buddhist tradition, practice is through meditation. The capacity to be present, living deeply each moment of our lives, is only found through meditation. Mindfulness is the fruit of meditation and allows us to be alive in the present moment, with our body and mind united. Faith and love are made up of direct experience. As direct experience grows, it produces freedom, enlightenment, and transformation. These are only found through deep looking inward to accept the suffering and confusion within you. Mindfulness allows us to touch life with healing, helping to transform afflictions into joy and freedom, as well as enabling you to look deeply at others and see their struggle as well.

Life is only available in the present moment, the Buddha teaches. If you are distracted, then your mind and body are not together and you will miss your appointment with life.

Joy and freedom are not found in gaining more stuff. The Haitian people are happier despite having less, and this is what Jesus taught in Mark 10:25, which states that "It is easier for a camel to pass through the eye of a needle than for one who is rich to enter the kingdom of God." After going on a pilgrimage to Israel as an adult, I got to actually see what He was referring to. There were several narrow passageways through the wall of Jerusalem, each called the eye of a needle. My group walked through one, a single person at a time. We had to have our backpacks passed through, never mind fitting an entire camel!

True freedom is only discovered when you see the eyes of Christ in other people and serve them in whatever way you can, always being joyful that God is the source and provider of life. It is important to take the time to spend with the people you love, because as the Buddha taught, all we have is the present moment. Don't waste that time living in the past or worrying about the future.

LITTLE HAITIAN BOY

open sores

bloated belly

gaunt limbs

cracked, bare feet

little Haitian boy
sleeps on dirt floor
runs naked through the days
laughs and plays
despite the destitution
that is his life
that is his future
that is his death...
hope yet sparkles in his eyes

(16 years old)

CHAPTER FIVE

Reflections on Losing a Sister

> *"Beloved, we are God's children now; what we shall be has not yet been revealed. We do know that when it is revealed we shall be like Him, for we shall see Him as He is."*
> 1 John 3:2

In this chapter I am going to talk about my experiences with my younger sister, Candi. As I mentioned earlier, she had hydrocephalus. Because of the excess cerebrospinal fluid that her brain was producing, her head got bigger, the pressure increasing and pushing her eyes down until you could see the whites above her eyes (a condition sometimes called half-moon eyes).

Candi was six months old before the doctors were finally able to diagnose her. Once they knew she had hydrocephalus, they immediately took her into surgery to insert a narrow piece of tubing, called a shunt, into the fluid-filled ventricle. The tubing then passed under the skin, draining the fluid into her abdomen. I remember every time she would have a growth spurt, the shunt tubing would pull on her brain tissue, causing severe headaches and swelling. Each time the neurosurgeon would add more tubing to temporarily fix the problem.

When I was two or three my dad and grandparents brought me to the hospital to visit her, following one of her many brain surgeries. They had shaved off her thick, wavy brown hair on half her head, leaving the stitches from the surgery visible. I thought the sutures down the side of her head were bees, and I was terrified for her.

"She's got bees all over her head! You gotta take off the bees! There's so many bees!!" Our pediatrician, Dr. Glasgow, was amazed at the level of understanding and compassion I showed Candi, though I was just a toddler myself.

The story of the bees is kind of funny to me now. When I learned to do sutures in medical school, I have to admit, they do kind of look like bees! After having my own set of stitches on my head, several times over, I guess it kind of is like bees buzzing around in there too. Or, at least that's how I experienced it.

Unfortunately, I didn't spend a lot of time playing with Candi when we were young because there were so many things she just couldn't understand. Once Rob arrived, the two of them became inseparable: two peas in a pod. I was older and busy pursuing what was important to me, which kept me from taking the time to notice all the things they were learning together.

I do remember how innocent and loving she was. One time while riding the bus to her elementary school, one of the older boys asked her if she was a virgin. She responded with, "Pff, no! I'm Italian!" Sweet Candi didn't know any better, which, in my opinion, is a beautiful thing. I long for my own kids to stay sheltered from life's adversity for as long as possible.

When I was 14, Candi had already had two prior surgeries that year before she was admitted with her final headache. She would have tremendous pain and swelling in her head that would signal to my parents that she needed to go to the hospital. Candi would have intense headaches, yet when my parents would ask how she felt, she would always say, "I'm a little bit fine." We eventually learned what that really meant was, "It hurts extremely bad!", although she was always hoping the pain would eventually ease. I have pretty severe migraines, but I cannot imagine what it would feel like to have a shunt pulling inside my brain. Candi, though, would always thank the doctors and nurses when they came in to do a procedure, take her vitals, or draw blood. She always saw the good in whatever was happening.

This time, though, Candi had a leak of spinal fluid, which had been confirmed by Dr. Glasgow, a few months before. Then, in late October, her head started to swell again. When my mom brought her to the pediatrician's office, there was a new doctor who told her that Candi was fine. When Mom asked for a second opinion, he said he was the only doctor there. Mom reluctantly brought Candi home, and my parents watched her closely in the days following.

Eventually her headaches got so bad, my parents knew she needed to go to the hospital. There she was diagnosed with pneumococcal meningitis, a bacteria that up until that point had only been known to cause pneumonia. The doctors called hospitals around the U.S., as well as Canada and Europe (this was before the internet), to see what other doctors had found to be the best treatment for it. However, this was a type of meningitis that no one had ever seen in the brain before. When I learned about the different types of meningitis in medical school, 10 years later, my professor said pneumococcal meningitis is still incurable today.

We learned years later that because Candi's head had gotten so large, the numerous surgeries in the exact same spot had stretched her skin, which allowed the bacteria to enter her brain. Because of what happened with her, neurosurgeons learned to be more careful about not using the same site when the patient would require multiple surgeries.

This was the first time that Candi was sick enough that I actually started to wonder if she was going to make it. My mom also says that it was the first time all three of us—my dad, my brother, and I—asked her if she thought that Candi would come home. "I don't know," she recalls telling each of us, nearly despairing.

The doctors started pushing multiple antibiotics directly into the spinal fluid in her brain, as well as intravenously, but each day Candi got worse. The day before she passed, she perked up a bit. She was smiling again, awake and talking with my mom and her mom. Gram was pleased to see that Candi was finally improving and decided to make the hour-long drive back home.

Mom says that she and Candi finally fell asleep around midnight. Exactly an hour later, my mom woke to code alarms, bright lights, and a room full of doctors and nurses. My sister had stopped breathing. They resuscitated and intubated her while my mom called my dad and our pastor. A few hours later, my parents felt the presence of God in the room and knew that my sister had transitioned from this world to her eternal home. After performing brain function tests, the doctors declared that she was brain dead. Candi was gone, exactly one week after being admitted to the hospital.

My parents decided to donate Candi's organs, and while they waited for the transplant team to do their tests, my dad came home to bring Rob and me to the hospital. At the age of 16, I wrote an essay about this experience that describes it in far more detail than what my jumbled brain could produce today. It's called "An Awakening," and I've included it here.

> "Aim, hurry! Get up! We've gotta go."

> At first, I was startled and rather confused. Why is my dad waking me up at four in the morning? As soon as my bare feet touched the floor, I knew. My mind drifted to the hospital while I quickly pulled my clothes on. Is she going to make it?

> Sitting in the car watching the familiar houses and offices go by, to me the short trip seemed like an eternity. I reflected on all the times I should have gone to visit her but had stubbornly refused. Feelings of regret instantly filled my heart. I didn't want to believe the despairing thoughts that were rushing to my mind, but I felt overwhelmed by the cold realization that they could be true.

My dad was silent as the heavy metal doors of the elevator slowly closed out the bustling hospital lobby. During the endless ride to her floor, the stillness made me feel more and more nervous. Mom met us with an exhausted, downcast look on her face.

"Is she going to be alright?" I asked her.

After a long pause, my mom replied, "Honestly... I don't know this time."

I walked down a long hallway and carefully opened her door. The room was small and dimly lit, and as I approached her bed, I noticed how pale and weak she looked.

I will never forget standing beside her thinking how, more than anything, I wanted to see her get up and come home with us. I looked away, trying to collect some optimism, and then turned back and studied the intrusive machines that surrounded her. I held her soft, frail hand in mine and told her she was going to get better. My eyes welled with tears, which suddenly turned into sobs.

"You can't leave me now! Please, you have to get

better!" I pleaded.

Then I cried out, "She can't be dead. She's still breathing. She's still alive!"

But as I stood there watching her, with tears streaming down my face, my heart knew that what I had been fearing was true. My time with her had come to an end, for she was now ready to pass from this world to the next... a world where she would suffer no longer.

I started crying at that moment of recognizing Candi's death, realizing what an awful sister I had been. There were times I could have gone to visit her at the hospital but had "better" things to do. I could have listened to her more, supported more, loved her more. So many years I had pretty much ignored both my siblings when I should have been more involved. I know Candi saw me as a role model, but I'm afraid I hadn't provided a very good one.

I think everyone was flabbergasted and utterly shocked that she was gone. Every other time, she had always come home. She died on the 24th of October, just 4 days before her 13th birthday, for which she had been excitedly planning a party with her friends. So many of her friends from school, in both her amazing special needs class and her regular class, were overwhelmed with the shock of her death. They even decided to dedicate a page to her in the yearbook.

Grief was really hard for me to deal with. I was distraught: laughing one minute, crying the next. A lot of my friends didn't know what to say, so they avoided me all together. I started making harmful decisions: hanging out with "bad" friends, smoking, drinking. Anything to fill the void I was experiencing.

When I asked my dad if I could go see a counselor, he told me that he didn't believe in counselors because depression was from the devil. It was only after both of his parents died several years later that he experienced the same depression I was dealing with then. He actually came back and apologized later, because he finally understood that when you feel depressed, there's nothing you can do on your own to make it better. As it was, though, I was in college when I finally started seeing a counselor.

The congregation at our Protestant church were understanding for the first six months or so. After that, I started hearing people quietly question who in my family had an unrepented sin that had cost my sister her life. I could not understand what kind of God would do that. It certainly doesn't sound like the kind, loving God I thought I knew: to take Candi from us was vindictive and mean, and I just couldn't put the two together. I was really struggling with my faith. I knew that there was a God, so I wasn't agnostic or atheist. I also knew that none of us in my family had sinned; Candi had just died, which our church friends couldn't reconcile. So I left high school with a lot more questions about faith than answers.

I also stopped caring about high school. My GPA dropped, and I didn't apply to any colleges. Rob Morris, one of our family friends, visited during this time and said that maybe attending a Youth With A Mission (YWAM) Discipleship Training School (DTS) would be good for me. Although these initiatives exist around the U.S. and the world, he was one of the leaders at a DTS in southern Texas. He said that we would spend 3 months in Texas, learning about a very different God than the one I had been encountering, and then we would then go on a three-month outreach mission to another country.

I thought maybe DTS would help me understand who God really is, which I sorely needed because at the time, I didn't like Him very much. So I applied to DTS and got accepted. I drove from New York to Texas with my new friend Heather, who lived nearby and also got accepted to the program. Together we experienced DTS and Texas, both of which were new to us.

When we arrived in Texas, both of us thought it was really weird how everyone we passed greeted us with a rousing, "Howdy!" In New York, you just get to where you're going, careful to not make eye contact with anyone you pass. And the oddness continued – once we were settled in, we decided to get a few groceries at a nearby store. As soon as we walked in, I remember a woman asking me in a long Texas drawl, "Y'all need a buggy?" I was not familiar with people saying "y'all", and I had no idea what needing a "buggy" meant. (They're actually shopping carts, for those of you who don't know either!) Now, looking back at our DTS experience, I am grateful for all the things we learned both in the classroom and in the great state of Texas.

When the classes actually started, there was a huge cross in the front of our classroom. The leaders invited us to write down or find an object that represented something that we needed to turn over to the Lord, and then to put it into the cracks of the cross. After thinking about it for several weeks, I realized that I was carrying a grudge against God for taking my sister from me. When I slid my piece of paper admitting this into that large cross, a tremendous sense of relief washed over me.

During those first few days we also hiked into the woods where there was a cross with all of these sticks hammered into the ground around it. Each of us was given a stick, just like the classes before us, to write all the things in our life that we wanted to turn over to God or wanted a second chance at. On mine, I wrote about my doubt, distrust, and questioning God, as well as my need to believe that He has the perfect soulmate for me, and for Him to change my grief over my sister into something good.

The woods were so quiet and still that I began hiking out there whenever I needed to think – when I needed to be closer to God in the silence. I also started reading Henry Nowen's book, *The Way of the Heart*, in which I learned that the silence is where we meet God. This was exactly what I needed to hear at that point. I started to love being in the quiet of the woods, where instead of talking to God, I would listen for His voice. I wrote many poems at the foot of that large cross; about Candi's death and processing the things going on in my mind. There were also poems written about the loneliness I felt, about the pain I had experienced, and about the God who loves me through it all. Each poem encapsulated a meaningful part of my life journey.

Heather and I both decided to spend our three-month outreach trip in Guatemala. When we were there, as always, I felt closer to God while helping others. This lesson, first learned in Haiti and reinforced in Guatemala, has stayed with me throughout my life. I became confident of my call to support the poor, the elderly, and the less advantaged in any way I can.

My DTS experiences helped me to see that God is a loving God—the one I already knew, and not the vengeful God that people in my home church had painted Him to be. Throughout DTS, I experienced great healing from the deep wounds that Candi's death had left behind. I also learned to discern when God is speaking and what isn't from Him.

Now when I think of Candi, I experience peace, joy,

and gratitude. I often wonder what it would be like to still have a sister, because although the wounds heal, they never go away completely. I think she would be proud of my life with Adam, and I know she would have loved my children very much. Each time I reminisce about a fond memory of her to my kids, I keep her spirit alive, helping them see they have an aunt who lovingly and protectively looks down on them from Heaven.

ODE TO MY SISTER

Her soft giggles
Drifted through the air
Light and cheerful
Like water gently flowing
Along a babbling brook

Her lighthearted nature
Spread joy and happiness to all
Like the pure delight
A playful puppy brings
To a small child

Her sunny disposition
Was gentle yet isolated
Like one fragile daisy
Standing proud
In a vast meadow

Her bright smile
Was peaceful and refreshing
Like the encompassing warmth
And relaxing tranquility
Of a summer day

(17 years old)

NEVER AGAIN

Your dark eyes gently close
As you fall into a deep eternal sleep
The sparkle slowly fades -
Never to be seen again.

My heart cries out to you
Pleading for your return
But you are leaving forever -
Never to come home again.

As I touched your hand
I wanted you to play and be a child,
But you were so still and cold -
Never to breathe with life again.

I miss you deeply day after day,
Emptiness aches inside me,
But you are now in heaven -
Never to feel pain again.

(14 years old)

CHAPTER SIX

Reflections on My Spiritual Journey

"Beloved, let us love one another, because love is of God; everyone who loves is begotten by God and knows God. Whoever is without love does not know God, for God is love."
1 John 4:7-8

After spending three months at Discipleship Training School (DTS) and three months on an outreach mission to Guatemala, I was accepted to Gannon University in a miraculous way that I will talk about further in a later chapter.

During the six months I spent waiting for school to start, though, both of my dad's parents, who I had been very close to, passed away. My Gram died first. She went to the Canadian side of Niagara Falls with my Grampa and another couple to celebrate Grampa's birthday. At the beginning of the day, they went to see the falls and take pictures together: there are even a few photos of just my Gram from that day. The other couple was driving back to the hotel, but as they turned left to enter the inn's parking lot, they were blindsided by a motorcyclist going almost 90 miles an hour. He was furthest to the curb, racing five other cyclists. When the motorcycle hit the back-passenger side of the car, my Gram was pushed into my Grampa's arms where she and the cyclist were both killed instantly.

The whole thing was so hard because she didn't die of old age: she was killed, and moreover, on my Grampa's birthday too. The pain exceeded what I thought I could bear. I missed her terribly, and I was not the only one. My normally cheerful Grampa became sad and sullen. Whenever we'd visit, he would sneak down to the basement and cry because he missed her so much. He stopped taking his heart medications, and on a 90+ degree day in June, he went out to mow his lawn, pushing himself far beyond what he could handle. He collapsed in the heat and after an ambulance brought him to a nearby hospital, they said his heart gave out in what they called "broken heart syndrome." My Grampa literally could not continue to exist without the woman he had loved for over 50 years.

Losing both grandparents in a matter of months brought back all of the questions and doubts that I'd felt when my sister died. And those doubts were very much still there when I embarked on my next big journey of college.

With all of this weighing on me, I entered Gannon, a Catholic University, with a very unsettled view of who God was. I didn't know if I could trust His "plan" for me if it was going to end up like it had for the people I loved, many of whom died for what seemed to me like no reason. When I got there, what I noticed almost immediately was that the Catholic students and staff saw I was struggling and wanted to know why. I never got the unsettled looks that my Protestant friends gave me; instead, the people at Gannon simply listened with compassion, wanting to hear my complex story and giving me the space to tell it. I felt known in a way that I had never experienced in my home church.

At DTS just a few months before, I had fallen in love with Henri Nouwen's work, and since then, I'd also gotten several more of his books. I was sad that he had died just before I learned of his work, because I loved the way he explained God's work in our lives. When I brought him up to a young woman working in Campus Ministry at Gannon, she said that I had to meet Father George, who had known Nouwen well and in fact officiated his funeral. I was very intrigued! A few days later, she and I were talking in a parking lot when out walked Father George. My friend introduced us with great excitement, and I was initially interested in him for what he could tell me about Henri Nouwen.

I stopped by his office to chat the following week, and the rest is history! I started sharing more and more personal information about my life with Father George, telling him that I often felt uncomfortable talking with people my age because they had not been through what I had and often misunderstood what I was saying. He told me something that only now has started to make sense. He said, "You do not have to look outside yourself for the answers. Everything you need to know is already within you." At the time, however, I was really confused by what he meant.

We kept meeting, though, and I appreciated the depth to which he could genuinely hear what I was saying. I started to wonder if going to Catholic Mass would further help me to understand what Father George had meant by saying what I was looking for was already within me. When I did begin attending, I found that the Mass was very liturgical, something I was not familiar with from the Protestant churches of my youth. The sermons (or homilies, as we Catholics call them) that Father George gave were always about a God of love who wants the very best for us. Sometimes he would even take his message further, saying that we need to spend time with God in the silence in order to see His constant presence and to hear Him communicate with us.

When it came time for communion during that first Mass I attended, which Catholics refer to as Eucharist, I was amazed to learn that Catholics have communion each time there is a Mass. In my home church, they offered white bread cut into squares and little cups of grape juice that we would partake in quarterly to symbolically commemorate Jesus' death and resurrection, but the Catholic Mass always includes the entire ritual.

The Catholic Church regards the Mass in which the Eucharistic blessing occurs as a sacrificial re-enactment of Christ's death on the cross. The priest "stands in" for Christ, who is both the high priest and sacrificial victim. Catholics believe that once the sacrament of bread and wine are blessed by a priest, the bread actually becomes the body of Christ and the wine becomes His blood.

Jason Evert, a Catholic author, said it well in his article, *Is The Mass a Sacrifice?* on Catholic.com: "[Jesus] appears in heaven in the state of a victim not because he still needs to suffer but because for all eternity He re-presents Himself to God appealing to the work of the cross, interceding for us, and bringing the graces of Calvary to us.

Moreover, Evert adds: "The Mass is a participation in this one heavenly offering. The risen Christ becomes present on the altar and offers himself to God as a living sacrifice. Like the Mass, Christ's words at the Last Supper are words of sacrifice, 'This is my body. . . this is my blood. . . given up for you.' So, the Mass is not repeating the murder of Jesus, but is taking part in what never ends: the offering of Christ to the Father for our sake,"

The more I observed this, the more I found myself wanting to participate in the miracle of Christ's death and resurrection that was happening right before my eyes. Having the ability to consume Jesus into yourself, I was realizing, would then give Him the power to heal all of the brokenness that lies within.

As I continued to attend Catholic Mass and meet with Father George, I also started to see that what Protestants call "denominations" were actually divisions within the church. If we are all called to live with love and harmony with each other, then it didn't (and still doesn't!) make sense to me that a church would be divided over the color of the song book or the slightest difference in interpretation of a scripture passage. If we are really following what Jesus said while He was on earth, then we should take what we hear from Saint Paul in 1 Corinthians 1:10 to heart: "I urge you, brothers [and sisters], in the name of our Lord Jesus Christ, that all of you agree in what you say, and that there be no divisions among you, but that you be united in the same mind and in the same purpose."

This was not the only change for me, though. Throughout my time at Gannon, I also became friends with several students from India. They practiced their Hindu faith in every part of their life: who they spent time with, what they ate, how they dressed, and more. In fact, it seemed they were much more dedicated to their beliefs than a lot of the Christians I knew. My Protestant friends back home believed that everyone besides members of their particular faith (including Catholics) would go to hell. Even before I came to Gannon, I just could not accept that, and here my experience just confirmed that belief even further for me. The Hindu students, for instance, showed love and kindness to everyone around them. There was no way that a loving God would shun them to hell. In fact, I thought they deserved to be in heaven all the more!

I appreciated that the Catechism of the Catholic Church (a summary of the beliefs of the Catholic faithful in book form), acknowledges the goodness and truth found in other religions. CCC #842 says, "The Church's bond with non-Christian religions is in the first place the common origin and end of the human race: All nations form but one community. This is so because all stem from the one stock which God created to people the entire earth, and also because all share a common destiny, namely God. His providence, evident goodness, and saving designs extend to all. . ." How Catholics see others, with love and acceptance, gave me a great deal of comfort in a God of perfect love, who would never abandon a person based on religion so long as they are seeking Truth.

In the fall of my junior year, I decided that I wanted

to become a Catholic myself. I went through the Rite of Christian Initiation of Adults (RCIA) program, led by Father George and Deacon Steve. When the day actually came for me to be joined with the rest of the Catholic family in receiving the body and blood of Christ, I was overwhelmed with the Divine power that descended upon me then and that continues to be with me to this day.

Often, after I receive Eucharist, I kneel back at my seat with tears running down my face. It's hard to believe, even now, that Jesus desires to enter me in such a powerful way. After I receive Him, it is easier for me to be loving to the people around me because it's Christ's love that I am radiating, not my own.

My fiancé Adam was confirmed the next year for his own reasons, and we got married in that same Catholic church by Father George just two years later. My friendship with Father George has continued for over 20 years now. He has gone through much of our life story with us, spiritually supporting Adam and I as well as our family each difficult step of the way.

However, my spiritual journey does not stop with Catholicism as the endpoint. In fact, it is quite the opposite. My journey is made up of so many encounters with a Higher Power in many different ways: in the church of my youth, in Candi's passing, in Discipleship Training School (DTS), in the death of my grandparents, in the service trips I went on, in the many diverse friends I made at Gannon, in Leadership and Discipleship in the Wilderness (LDW), in conversations with friends, in spending time outdoors, in marriage and raising children together, and in learning and practicing the medicine I love. All these different events and experiences have revealed to me the face of Christ through the people whose paths I crossed.

In learning about Buddhist and Contemplative Christian meditation, I realized the importance of resisting notions about God in order to have direct experience with Him. Father George continues to teach me today that in meditation, what he said to me so long ago is now all the more true: "Everything you need to know is already within you." I see now that, by being fully present in the moment, I can heal the suffering within myself while also helping those around me. Looking inward to my Beloved-self and living out of that love has been the calling of my life. My hope is that you will also discover your calling as you encounter the Beloved within yourself in meditation.

Behind your eyes
exists an isolated land,
a desolate world through which
you travel alone...

I give myself to you
unfalteringly
with hope that you will
allow me inside,
that you will someday realize
the strength of my love
to gaze upon your darkness
and never turn away...

In this shelter
built on my unfailing love
you are safe
to reveal that deep place:
your beautiful dreams,
your disfiguring scars,
the core of your soul...

My heart will always
embrace you.

(20 years old)

CHAPTER SEVEN

Reflections on Marriage

"I am my Beloved's and my Beloved is mine."
Song of Songs 6:3

I spent the summer break between my sophomore and junior years of college backpacking in the Wind River Range of Wyoming. When I came back to school after that experience, I decided to spend my time investing in my relationship with God rather than, in my words at the time, pursuing some stupid guy for another pointless relationship. Gannon University was very preppy at the time, and after my trip, I spent more time hanging out with the small hippie crowd: a dread-locked, makeup-free, unshaven, hacky sack-playing, hemp jewelry-wearing group of people who accepted the new me.

One day soon after school started, I was eating lunch with one of my friends on the second floor of our new college building whose outdoor walls were floor to ceiling windows. We were watching the freshmen pass by on the sidewalk below that led to their dorm. One of the guys walking by was wearing a cut-off flannel shirt hanging over navy blue work pants and a navy bandana tied around his head. He appeared kind of hippie-ish, and from where I was sitting, he was pretty good-looking too.

It was a good first impression, but I quickly let it go. *You're focusing on yourself right?*, my brain reminded me.

When fall break came in mid-October, I was desperate to get back out into the woods. At the time, it seemed like that was the only place where everything made sense. There was a school group going to the Dolly Sods in West Virginia, and I immediately signed up along with several of my new friends. One of them told me that the guy I had had my eye on was going too, and in case I was interested, his name was Adam.

As it turned out, Adam and I were riding in the same van, and the first thing I noticed then was how he had a strong opinion about everything. We had a big discussion about selective logging versus clear-cutting, which, after being in the woods for nearly the whole summer, I was opposed to logging in any form. (Funnily enough, we later ended up having our 70-acre Vermont property undergo selective logging in order to make room for the more expensive trees to grow for higher future income that now the new owners will take advantage of. The irony of it all!)

I asked Adam what his last name was, and he replied: "Knauff." I was confused by the word I'd heard, though. With what was probably a bewildered look on my face, I repeated, "Mouth? Elf? Naulf?" trying to understand what he had said.

Adam was very gracious about my confusion, though, telling me: "Here, maybe it will help if I spell it: K-n-a-u-f-f." I thought that sounded like a mouthful, but I didn't say so, just: "Ah, ok!" I never expected that this would also be my last name 4 years later!

When we got to Dolly Sods, the leaders divided us into two hiking groups. I was in one group and Adam was in the other. They said we would meet in the middle of our hike for dinner and to sleep and then cross paths again the next day. During this experience, I really liked how comfortable Adam was with people who were older and further along in their college experience than he was. He didn't mind snuggling in with us and even let us put wildflowers in his hair. He was also funny, even irreverent: at one point, he walked up to my friend Eve, also a junior, and said, "You know, every Eve needs an Adam!" Although she was not amused, the rest of us found it hysterical!

Adam and I talked nearly the whole bus ride to West Virginia, a lot that evening while we were there, and then for the entire bus ride home. In some ways, it seemed that we had lived parallel lives and we had a very similar outlook on life as well. After that trip, every time I saw him we would talk for hours, and before long we became fast friends. Looking back now, I believe having both a friendship beforehand and strong communication skills throughout will set you up for a lasting marriage.

Soon after the trip, I was sitting on the grass with my good friend Allie, telling her that Adam had all the characteristics that I would want in a husband. I later learned that, all the while, Adam was on the phone with his best friend, telling him the same thing about me. This was November 5, 2000. During our phone conversation later that evening, Adam and I both stumbled over our words as we shared our matching conversations with each other. I suggested we should talk more about this face to face, and he came over to my apartment a few minutes later.

Now let me backup for a minute. After I graduated from high school, I had started to pray even more to find my husband, my soulmate, especially while at Discipleship Training School (DTS). On our three-month outreach to Guatemala, where I turned 18, I wrote poem after poem about finally meeting this soulmate and how our lives would join into one. I also found this verse: Proverbs 31:30

which states, "Charm is deceptive and beauty is fleeting; the woman who fears the Lord is to be praised." Wow! This described what I wanted perfectly: a man who would love me more for what's inside than for how I looked. I asked God that when I find the perfect man, he would read this verse to me.

Ok, back to the story at hand.

That night, after our stumbling phone conversation, Adam walked into my apartment and said that he had come across a Bible passage that he wanted to read to me. The whole time I was thinking: "What if he reads my verse? *What if he reads my verse??*"

Which, of course, is what he did.

As he read this verse, I sat there staring at him, unable to speak. Then he started quoting – yes, I did say quoting – a poem that I had written on a Guatemalan motel balcony almost three years before. No one had ever seen my journal, yet Adam was now saying the first part of that very poem almost exactly word for word as I had written it.

I stood up, shaking my head in disbelief, and walked over to the bookshelf to get the journal. When I opened it up and showed him the page, he read the poem out loud:

TWO IMMORTAL SOULS

That which comes
from your hand

could be nothing less
than perfect,
awe-inspiring,
Sublime.
Even when you talk
of nothing
our souls commune
as one.
Even in absence,
your presence is felt
closer than my
Skin.
Love for you
engulfs my heart,
mind,
soul
completely.
The marriage of our
two immortal souls
cannot be broken
by time and space,
but will live
strong
for all eternity.

When he was done, he just sat and stared at me with bewilderment. I then told him how God had shown me that

I would marry the man who shared the verse he had just read to me. We silently stared at each other, both starting to tear up. Then we said in unison, "I think I'm supposed to marry you," before falling into each other's arms. We couldn't believe what had just happened and decided to go share the news with a few of our friends, who were equally surprised. Not nearly as surprised as Adam's mother, however!

Over Thanksgiving break, we got such a bad snowstorm that they closed the highway I would have needed to go home. Adam said that I could go home with him to meet his family and to see the house he grew up in. I agreed, and about 30 minutes later, we were in the car, headed south for the hour-and-a-half hour drive to his home.

When we finally arrived, his mom, dad, and "Pappy" were all there waiting to meet me. Adam introduced me: "This is Aimee, the woman I'm going to marry."

His mom was taken aback, "Yeah right!" she exclaimed. "You find someone new every month! We'll see if this WOMAN" – she used air quotes here – "is going to stick around! I don't think you fully know yourself, never mind what you want in a wife."

We all have a good laugh now when the story is brought up, because 20 years later, I'm still here!

Adam and I were hoping to get married that summer, because we knew we were meant to be together. There were obstacles in the way, though, because he had three more years of school to go, while I would be a senior next year. We tried to discuss this idea with his mom and dad, but both of them vigorously shook their heads, saying "No! You're not doing that!"

His dad sternly reminded Adam, "I have a plan for you," and then proceeded to write it out: Graduate High School, Go to College, Get a Job, Get Married. Adam looked at his dad and said, "What if I want to change your 'plan' for me?"

To which his dad responded adamantly, "NO! I don't accept that!" Then, after taking a few deep breaths, he calmed down enough to say: "If you guys get married while you're still in school, that's fine, but all our financial help is done." That grabbed our attention; at the time, neither of us had anywhere near full-time employment. After further discussion, Adam's dad finally agreed to switch the last two parts of the plan, and we agreed to wait to have our wedding after Adam graduated.Because Adam and I were engaged for nearly four years, we started to think that our wedding was more a confirmation to everyone else of what we already knew: that we were destined to be together. We met with Father George for premarital counseling, and our love for each other became clear to him as well. He agreed that we were meant for each other and was looking forward to celebrating our wedding with us.

Then, the day before Adam's college graduation, I was diagnosed with a brain tumor. It was a huge blow to both of us, but it didn't change our love for one another and we decided to still go through with the wedding as planned. In fact, the vows we exchanged on our wedding day rang even more true, knowing what we had just learned: "I, Aimee, take you, Adam, for my lawful husband, to have and to hold from this day forward, for better, for worse, for richer, for poorer, in sickness and health, until death do us part." Both of us had tears in our eyes as we repeated these words, not knowing how my brain surgery the following month would affect us. We definitely didn't know then that there would be four more tumors, three more surgeries, radiation, and chemotherapy, not to mention the tremendous impact that each one of these things would have on our relationship.

We went on our honeymoon to Hershey, Pennsylvania, and a few weeks later, in July of 2004, the best neurosurgeon at Hamot hospital, where I worked, performed the surgery. I didn't appear to have any side effects from the procedure, and the Erie neurosurgeon, Dr. G said the pathology results came back as a grade 2 astrocytoma that was growing very slowly. He thought he got it all and sent me with a script to have a follow-up MRI in Arizona in six months. Adam and I excitedly packed up our apartments and the next month we were on our way to Phoenix in pursuit of my medical school dream. Yes, I know: this sounds crazy to me now too!

We remained friends with Father George, who we discovered attended a five-day silent retreat in Tucson twice a year. He would fly into Phoenix, stay at our condo for a couple of days, go to his retreat, and then spend the night in our guest room before flying home the next day. God knew that with each trip Father George took, he would always come exactly when we needed to see him the most. He was there to help us through each pregnancy, each birth, each tumor surgery.

Adam has always been a wonderful support, with my surgeries, pregnancies, all of it. He was my rock, always there for me, always a fantastic support system and we made it all work. However, Adam slowly started taking on more and more household responsibility; because of my condition, because of med school, because of our kids, because of my busy medical practice, etc. – all reasons someone had to step up to keep things moving. I slowly gave more and more responsibility to Adam, and over time he silently accepted each one.

He lost his job right after our first child, Sofia, turned one, so after much discussion we decided that he should stay home to watch her while we lived off just my college loans. I admit, I was not easy for Adam to be around at the time. I would be mentally "on" at the clinic all day, friendly to everybody else, but when I got home, I was completely exhausted from the day. I became mean, angry, grumpy, rude, and miserable with Adam, when he had done nothing to deserve it.

Because I felt secure in our marriage vow, I knew that Adam would always be there for me. Unfortunately, because

I couldn't take my anger out on God, I took it out on him instead. Sometimes even my kids caught a glimpse of my fury. I was also unable to see that Adam needed support too: that he was struggling with my brain surgeries and the aftermath as much as I was. I wasn't a good example of a loving wife because I couldn't see past my own pain. I couldn't see how important it was to support him in the same way he had supported me all these years.

I kept telling Adam, "I just need to get through medical school and board exams. Once we move back east, I promise everything will be better." And life really did get much better after I graduated, passed my boards, and we moved to Vermont.

Because of my prior three surgeries, I had gotten into the mindset that I would die from brain cancer. When my MRI's were good for so long in Vermont, I started to imagine what my long-term future would look like with Adam. I pictured us being old and retired, thinking about what we would do and what the world would look like then. For the first time I really started to imagine both of us with grey hair, being the cute old couple still in love after all these years.

This clarified things for the kids too. A few years back, all three of my children came up to me and Sofia asked, "Mama, which one of us do you love the most?" Each of them gestured to themselves.

I answered, "I love Papa the most."

She tried to correct me: "No, I mean out of us kids, which one of us do you love the most?"

Again I replied, "Papa."

They were a bit perplexed by my answer, so I explained further. "I will always love you three because you are a part of me. My heart was made to love you. Papa is different. I have to choose, every day, to be with him. You will all grow up and leave us to live your own lives. I don't want Papa to be a stranger from years of growing apart. I want to love him even more than I did on our wedding day." The three of them shook their heads as they walked away.

A month later, they asked me the same question, and I gave them the same answer. Then, when they asked me the third time, I think they finally understood what I was telling them: the most important thing I have learned in my marriage is that you have to choose, each day, to love the person you are with. When life gets busy and crazy and difficult – especially then, in fact – it is so important to have the love and support that only your spouse can provide. Having a partner who is your biggest cheerleader, who always wants you to succeed, is the best motivation there is. They watch your back as you watch theirs. When things get tough, you can confide in your spouse who has committed to be with you "till death do us part."

In November 2015, my fourth tumor reared its ugly head. On the MRI, it was much smaller than the ones I'd had previously: about the size of a pea. It also didn't enhance, meaning it did not yet have blood supply. So I asked my Arizona neurosurgeon, Dr. Kris Smith, if I could get through the holidays with my family before coming in for surgery. He agreed.

After this fourth surgery, there were so many things that I needed to re-learn. I really appreciated having my "mother-in-love" with me in Arizona, helping me figure out how to do stuff again after the surgery, and always in gentle ways. For example: When I was still in the hospital, I could not remember what to do after I went to the bathroom. I finally looked at her with utter confusion, and she tenderly offered, "Maybe you'd like to wash your hands?" She also helped me re-learn how to dress, bathe and other activities of daily living with compassion and understanding. I was so grateful to have her in Arizona with me.

When I got home, I had to be shown how to walk up and down stairs, how to do laundry, etc. I could only do one task at a time or else I would lose track of what I was doing. For instance, Sofia always wanted to talk to me while I was in the kitchen. I finally learned to tell her, "All of my focus right now is on getting these dishes put away. If you can wait five minutes, you'll have my complete attention."

The doctors said to avoid driving until they had seen me again in six months and could verify that it was safe for me to operate a vehicle. This meant that I could no longer get our three kids to where they needed to be. I could no longer go grocery shopping, coach Sofia's soccer team, participate in school activities the kids were involved in, or go to speech therapy on my own. So Adam assumed all of the family responsibilities yet again, leaving him little free time for anything he wanted to do.

He also started to really miss the Pennsylvania home of his youth. So, in December of 2016, we left behind my dreams of living in Vermont in pursuit of being closer to his family and friends for support. We found a smaller home in Pennsylvania, and my brother's family and my mother also moved out here in the years that followed.

I've come to see that to truly love someone is to deeply listen to them. For me, this means that my perspective can't be the only thing that controls how I act towards Adam. He wanted to move back home, and I finally saw how lonely he had been in Vermont. I can see now that the more I can deeply listen to what he's been through and what he's going through, it better allows me to truly support him where he is. This means to want the very best for him, knowing he has always been there for me, and without serving my needs first. I admit that I haven't done a good job of this before now, and I still feel very sorry for the suffering I have caused him.

When we heard that I had a fifth tumor in the beginning of 2019, it felt like Adam turned his back on me. He made sure that the kids were taken care of, because he's always been a fantastic caregiver, but he left me out. It seemed like he just couldn't deal with another diagnosis, more disabilities, and for the first time ever, I felt like I had to face my cancer alone. It was a lonely road at the beginning because I didn't know where he was and what I needed to do to get him back. Adam is my everything; I cannot imagine life without him. However, I started to feel less and less like I was *his* everything in return.

When we finally had a conversation about this, he told me, "If I could go back in time, I don't even know if we should have gotten married. I'm going to stick it out because that's what married people do, but if I had it do it all over again, I don't know if I would have chosen you." Whoah; that was very hard to hear. However, we are still married, and we committed to always work things out. You certainly have to be good at forgiving and asking for forgiveness to be in a lasting marriage!

What can I do to make myself more open? What do I need to change? What are things I need to ask forgiveness for? What do I need to forgive? These are questions that I have asked myself many times over the past year.

Every Monday morning, Father George and I do a video call for about an hour. After my fifth diagnosis, I shared with him how difficult I was for Adam to be with in Arizona. I wondered aloud if that was why Adam chose to withdraw from me now, despite the pain it was causing us both. I had never realized that by slowly giving up more of my responsibilities, it was putting more and more work on Adam. By being so consumed with my own pain, I had been unable to really acknowledge the pain that Adam was dealing with.

Father George introduced me to the work of the Zen Buddisht monk and prolific author, Thích Nhat Hanh. The first of his books that we read together was *True Love: A Practice for Awakening the Heart*, which has helped me to become more centered. Fixing my marriage all starts with me, for as Nhat Hanh teaches: "The object of your practice should first of all be yourself. Your love for the other, your ability to love another person, depends on your ability to love yourself."

He also teaches that to "be there is the first step, and recognizing the presence of the other is the second step. To love is to recognize; to be loved is to be recognized by the other." From this I learned that I am truly present in the moment, I can deeply listen to what Adam or other loved ones are saying, good or bad. In Buddhist meditation, your mind becomes free of the thoughts that float by and you can just be present. Or, as Father George put it to me: "By being present in the moment, you can then meet the 'I AM' that is within you, and you can be present for the people around you. You can be more present to notice different things around you that you have the power to change."

I feel like this is a lesson we could all learn: how to be present in the current moment through meditation and genuinely listen to what is being said by the loved ones around us. To truly listen is to truly love.

I have had several difficult conversations with Adam over the past few months, trying to really listen to what his struggles with me are. I have learned, for instance, that he has always been a caregiver to me, but also that it was not a reciprocal caregiving based on mutual love. This has its place in Thích Nhat Hanh's teachings too, particularly that "True love always brings joy to ourselves and to the one we love. If our love does not bring joy to both of us, it is not true love." Although I do love Adam, more today than ever before, it is only recently that I realized how caregiving is a mutual expression of love - you each give care to the other. Adam has to feel as supported and encouraged as he has made me feel. This is something I am working on: treating Adam with compassion and love instead of anger or apathy, as I have inadvertently been doing for a very long time.

All of this comes easier now as I continue to find my Beloved-self in meditation, and in healing my suffering, I can be more attentive to heal his suffering as well. Thích Nhat Hanh maintains that there's no use in worrying about the past and the future. You can look ahead, but the future is made of a compilation of the now, all of these current moments strung together. According to Nhat Hanh's teachings: "Live your best in the current moment and the future's memories will be good." Although there is nothing I can do to change the past, I can make our future memories better by being present in the current moment, continually encouraging Adam and our children to be their best selves.

Adam and I continue to work on communicating, which has always been our strong suit, but it's harder now because of my short-term memory loss. I forget what I've done during the day, who I've talked to, what I've said and what's been said to me. The most common thing people hear from me is, "Sorry, I can't remember," or "Sorry, I've forgotten if I already told you this." However, for Adam and I this has brought us into an even deeper understanding of love. We see now that when you truly love someone, you take the time to learn your partner's heart-song and sing it back to them when they forget. So many times, he is my voice when I can no longer remember the words, and I am confident that he will carry on my song to my family and friends, long after I am gone.

Alone
I sit and look out
Into the endless
Night sky

I wonder
Where you are
How you are
If you are thinking
Of me tonight

The future
Dark, unknown
Like the vast ocean
I gaze upon

When will our paths meet?
When will our dreams come true?

How I long
To see you
To sit and look out
Together

(17 years old)

CHAPTER EIGHT
Reflections on Brain Cancer

"Beloved: If you are patient when you suffer for doing what is good, this is a grace before God. For this you have been called, because Christ also suffered for you, leaving you an example that you should follow in his footsteps."
1 Peter 2:20b-21

To really understand brain cancer, it is also important to understand what a glioma is and what "grade" means. Glioma refers to a tumor arising from the glial group of cells in the brain, which surround and provide support for neurons (specialized cells that transmit nerve impulses). There are several kinds of gliomas, including astrocytomas and oligodendrogliomas, both of which have been found in my tumors. Meanwhile the term "grade" is used to classify tumors based on how aggressive they are. There are four grades of gliomas: grades 1 and 2 are slow-growing pre-cancerous tumors and grades 3 and 4 are both aggressively growing cancer.

When people hear about my diagnosis, they often ask me: "How are you still here?" This is because most people my age are diagnosed with Glioblastoma Multiforme (GBM), a very aggressive grade 4 tumor that tends to take over the brain in mere months. Patients with these tumors usually survive a year at most. *How am I still here?* I often wonder about that myself, 16 years after my initial diagnosis.

My brain tumor story began in the spring of 2004. I'd been having monthly migraines for an entire year prior. My boss at the Hamot Hospital lab where I worked suggested that I go to my doctor to see if I could get an FMLA certification through the Family and Medical Leave Act. This way, she could give me more time off than what my current paid time off (PTO) provided.

When I called to set up an appointment, the first doctor I could see was a resident, which I said was fine. On the day of the appointment, after exchanging pleasantries with her, the resident told me, "Looks like you've been on Imitrex [a migraine medicine] for an entire year, and it doesn't seem to really help you. Let's find out why you're having migraines." I agreed, thinking they probably should have done more to find the cause when I first presented with head pain. She scheduled a brain CT scan for the following day. When it lasted longer than the half-hour time it was supposed to take, I started growing concerned. Then after they scheduled me for a brain MRI, I knew that they must have seen something. And my suspicion was correct – the MRI scan had revealed a mass the size of a golf ball located in the left temporal-parietal lobes of my brain.

The resident called me after seeing the MRI findings and had to hold back her emotions as she told me, "It looks like you have a mass in the left side of your brain that they think might be cancer. You're so young," she continued, holding back tears. "I'm sorry this is happening to you. I made an appointment for you with Dr. G, our best neurosurgeon, early next week. If I were you, I'd pack a hospital bag because he might want to admit you for a biopsy right then."

By how she was acting, I'm pretty sure I was the first young person she had to give a probable cancer diagnosis to. And I *was* young for this kind of news – at 24 years old, the diagnosis came the day before Adam would graduate college and just a month before our wedding. I was in complete shock, but I agreed to go see the surgeon all the same.

The following week Adam and I went to the intake visit, where the Erie, Pennsylvania neurosurgeon told us, "There is a mass, but I can't tell you exactly what it is yet. Sometimes it is cancer, but it could also be multiple sclerosis or something else. What I'd like to do is admit you to the hospital and take a biopsy of the mass. We'll try to get the whole thing out while we're in there."

We explained our situation, and Dr. G agreed to wait until after our wedding to do the surgery. I signed the surgical consent form, which included death as a possible outcome. Then, on the day of surgery, Adam and my parents stayed in the prep room as the medical staff wheeled me down the hallway toward the operating room. I remember asking to hug my new husband one more time, not knowing if I would ever see him again.

After surgery, I woke up in the recovery room to find Adam sitting next to my bed, earnestly waiting to see how I was. It seemed to both of us that the surgery hadn't caused any noticeable side effects. Dr. G came in and said, "I think we got the entire mass. According to pathology, it's a grade 2 astrocytoma. You're lucky we caught it now. If we had waited for you to start having symptoms from the tumor, there's often nothing we can do at that point." I was relieved, but at the same time, still in shock about what had happened.

We moved to Arizona, where my six-month follow-up MRI showed half of the circular mass still remaining, which meant that the first neurosurgeon did not get all of it like he hoped. Adam and I knew the tumor was precancerous, though, so we made an appointment with Dr. Kris Smith, a neurosurgeon at Barrow Brain and Spine. We were excited to learn that Barrow Neurological Institute is a "World Class Destination for Neurosurgery" and just so happened to be located in Phoenix. I met several people who had also had brain surgery there, and all of these previous patients said that their surgeons needed training in bedside manners. This left me wondering what to expect from Dr. Smith.

I am pleased to say, the neurosurgeon who took my case was phenomenal. Dr. Smith spends as much time as each patient needs, meaning that he always runs late. However, his patients know that once he was with them, their particular case was all he was thinking about. Dr. Smith answered all our questions, making sure we knew exactly what was going to happen. He performed my second surgery, as well as my third and fourth tumor resections. To this day, he is the only surgeon I trust to cut into my head because he uses minimally invasive surgery techniques with the patient's best interests in mind.

My second craniotomy went according to plan. When I asked Dr. Smith how the surgery went, he said that it all went fine. We assumed that meant everything was good to go. Tumor, done. Next on the checklist, medical school! How little we knew then...

After the surgery, I had a harder time finding words. When Dr. Smith told me that he had "gotten a clear margin," this was the medical way of saying, "I also took healthy tissue around the tumor." The reason I was having speech difficulty was because my tumor was located between Broka's and Wernicke's areas.

Let me explain what this means. A Wernicke's deficiency is called "word salad" because you are able to say words, but they don't string together to make sense. On the other hand, when Broka's area is impaired, you have "broken speech," where you can't say anything at all. I had a mix of the two. Here is an example of one the many embarrassing stories that my family still picks on me for:

> Adam sat down on the couch and was going to put his feet up on the ottoman when I declared, "Get your feet off the. . . fox!"
> He quizzically replied, "I don't know about no fox! Do you mean ottoman?"
> I replied, "Yeah, yeah, that's what I said!"
> Of course, I didn't realize that I had even said *fox* in the first place!

I was in my senior year of medical school, Sofia had just turned two, and our second child Everest was eight months old, when my MRI revealed a third tumor. When the new scan showed that not only had this tumor filled in its original space, but also that it had invaded the brain tissue around it, we feared it was no longer slow growing. Dr. Smith said we should take it out as soon as possible, so with just one semester of school left, I decided to put school on hold and have the surgery. And indeed, pathology indicated that the tumor was a mix of astrocytoma and oligodendrocytoma cells that had changed from a slow-growing grade 2 to a more aggressive grade 3.

When I woke up from this surgery, I noticed that along with the word-finding side effects I had expected, the entire right side of my body was also paralyzed. My surgeon confessed that during the surgery he had nicked a capillary that feeds the area of the brain that controls movement, causing me to have a stroke. After this, my friend Nina would come over to our condo and do a post-stroke acupuncture treatment several times a week. Little two-year-old Sofia would follow along behind her, putting imaginary needles into points on my skin, repeating with her sing-song voice what Nina was saying. Although it was a very difficult time, I still smile when I remember my "apupunture" sessions.

Although my gross motor movement came back in about a month, it took almost a year to regain most of my fine motor skills. Even now, if you really look at my face, you'll notice that the right side droops a bit. But it's my handwriting that was the most frustrating thing to lose and that has never fully returned. I have older journals and notebooks filled with beautiful writing; now all I wish for is that my chicken scratch is legible.

After this particular surgery, I had a big discussion with Adam, Dr. Smith, and my neuro-oncologist about how to further treat my cancerous tumor. At the time, a research study was currently being done comparing the results of different cancer treatments: radiation alone, chemotherapy alone, and patients getting both. This study showed a similar life expectancy with each of the three options, so it seemed like I could choose from among them. I was still hoping for a third baby at some point in the future, so I wanted to avoid chemotherapy in hopes of preserving my fertility. I said, "Why don't I do radiation now, leaving chemo as an option if the tumor comes back?" Everyone agreed.

After waiting a few weeks for my brain to heal, I started radiation therapy at a clinic 45 minutes away. My treatments were five days a week for six weeks. We couldn't afford for Adam to drive me because he was home watching our two kids after losing his job a few months before, so every weekday I called the state-run medical transportation that would provide me a ride to and from the clinic.

I have to be honest: radiation therapy is the most traumatic memory of this entire illness. Because they were using computer-pinpointed delivery, it was of the utmost importance that my head be in the exact same position every day. The first day they created a mask that was wrapped millimeters from my face, and then they screwed it down to the table upon my arrival for every treatment.

Although the treatment itself was only 15 minutes long, it took everything in me to stay still while they screwed my head down each day. I was lying on an open table, yet as the machine whirled around me, I felt so trapped. I would try to hum with the radio to clear my mind of what was happening, but that was not enough. I'm not usually claustrophobic, but boy did I dread enduring those 15 minutes of torture day after day.

I was also extremely fatigued after the treatment, and my hair started falling out during the second week. First the hair loss was right at the radiation site, then it started on the opposite side of my head as well. I remember standing at the bathroom sink having handfuls of hair fall out. By week three, I decided to shave my surgery-scarred head because I was losing so much hair, and Adam shaved his own head in solidarity. When I finished treatment, the staff understood my sharp "NO!" when they asked me if I wanted to keep my mask. To this day I am grateful for the kindness that the staff showed me, but I am also very happy that this particular treatment is in the rearview mirror.

I graduated in January, right in the middle of my radiation treatments. I insisted on getting a wig to wear at graduation because I didn't want to be the "bald, droopy-smiled cancer patient" in front of my classmates and all their loved ones. Now, looking back on the pictures, unfortunately I don't remember most of the big day, which I certainly never expected of my own graduation.

In medical school I learned to ask what my prognosis is – i.e., for a forecast of the likely course of my illness. What I really wanted to know was: how long does someone with my type of brain cancer usually live? When I asked this question to Dr. Smith, he told Adam and I that the longest he had seen a person with my diagnosis survive was 13 years. Most patients, though, have only a couple of years at best, because eventually the tumor evolves into grade 4 GBM. However, at the time of writing this in 2020, mine hasn't yet! In fact, this is my 16th year of living with a grade 3 tumor, and yes, that is a miracle in itself – a miracle that I am thankful for every day. It also demonstrates why is so important not to take a single day for granted: for me with brain cancer, and also for you with whatever you're struggling with.

But this is where I am today. At the time, I was very angry with God for giving me a brain with recurrent cancer, and also about the prognosis we had gotten. I had a family and a good life, and I was almost finished with a medical degree in a field that I loved. I just couldn't understand. The more I thought about it, the more furious I became, to the point of feeling enraged with God.

What did I do to deserve this? Why do the tumors keep coming back? Why was I married to a husband I loved and blessed with two beautiful children that I will someday have to leave behind? I really questioned how God can be a loving God and yet allow good people to get sick or die. All the questions and doubts from losing my sister and then my grandparents came flooding back, just as intense now as they had been then.

After I found out that I passed my boards, we moved to Vermont in December of 2010, right before the snow really set in. We also found a church that embraced us, and I began meeting with Father Peter, the local priest. We talked a lot about the why's of suffering, and I felt that he could understand what I was struggling with.

Father Peter was the one who told me this: "Suffering is never something that God gives us. He is perfect. He wants life and fullness, joy and happiness in our lives. He didn't bring disease to us. The reason we get diseases that are sometimes deadly is because we are broken people living in a broken world."

Father Peter also said that sometimes suffering is the only gift we have to offer. Or, as he put it: "When things get hard, ask God to come and be a part of what's going on. When you ask Him to take this burden away from you, He sometimes purposefully doesn't because He wants you to see Him in the suffering; to embrace Him in the suffering. When you know God is present in your affliction, you also start to see His hand guiding you in the good times as well. In good times and in bad, He is there. You start living life in a more joyful way, even when the pain isn't taken away, because you know God is on your side. This is how you can be joyful in your suffering."

My talks with Father Peter completely changed my understanding of suffering, and also of God's purpose in my suffering. I could finally turn around and see that God was always there, even when I was pushing Him away. He was reaching out to hold me the whole time. I think for me – and I wonder if maybe this is the case for you too – I just needed to stop. I was so tired of being angry and felt like I just couldn't do it anymore. My husband deserved better. My kids deserved better. I deserved better.

When they detected a fourth tumor on my MRI in November 2015, it was pea-sized, and it didn't enhance, meaning it didn't have blood supply yet. By this time, I also had many more things in my life than I had with the other three tumors: not only did I have a husband I loved, but now I also had three amazing children, a church and friends I cherished, and a thriving medical practice. After my previous experience, I didn't know whether or not I wanted to have any more surgeries.

I went in to talk with Father Peter about this, but he said he didn't know either – having someone cut into your head, even to give you a chance to heal, wasn't exactly a moral decision with a clear-cut answer. He suggested that I go with Adam to the prayer chapel and listen. God would always show us the way, he reminded me.

We did exactly what he said. The next day, Adam and I went to the adoration chapel. Sitting at kneelers next to each other, we both waited quietly and listened. I started to silently pray for God to show us what to do because I couldn't figure it out on my own. All of a sudden, I felt these huge arms wrap around me and pull me in for an embrace. I started crying because I knew He was there with us. He then clearly whispered, "Go." In my tears I responded quietly, "Ok, Lord. I will go." He then said, "Everything is going to be ok," to both of us at the same time. We left that day with the confidence that God would be with us every step of the way.

Dr. Smith in Arizona agreed to wait until after the holidays to do the surgery. Adam and I planned for me and his mom to fly out on my birthday, while he stayed home in Vermont to maintain normalcy for our three kids. Even though Adam, bless his heart, gave the flight attendants money to buy me drinks during the flight, it was the worst birthday of my life because I was so nervous about the upcoming surgery. After all, this tumor, instead of being in the temporal/parietal area like the others, was in front of the radiation scar seen on all the MRI's since the radiation therapy following surgery number three – meaning that the tumor was in my frontal lobe. This is the part of your brain that makes you the person you are. I was really nervous having them cut into my frontal lobe because I didn't know who I would be after the surgery.

When I got to Arizona with my "mother-in-love" (as Adam's mom says), the head neuropsychologist Dr. P did a whole panel of tests to identify a baseline before the surgery. I would then have another panel done six months post-surgery to see what had changed. After looking at where my mass was, Dr. P told me I would have problems with multitasking and with encountering a word that I didn't know. Before, especially at my medical practice, if I came to a word I couldn't remember, I would mentally run through similar words until I found a comparable one, all while listening to the patient, thinking of the next question to ask, and thinking of differential diagnoses and which lab tests to run. My brain felt like it was running a thousand miles per hour just to get through each conversation, explaining why I was so exhausted each day when I got home.

Dr. P said that, following this surgery, when I came to a word I didn't know, this would halt me because that word would simply be gone. He also said that multi-tasking would be a challenge, and that I would feel guarded and overwhelmed when there were a lot of people around. Likewise, he warned that I would have a harder time remembering things, as well as increased problems with working memory and mood regulation.

Pretty much everything he said corresponded exactly with the side effects that I felt. Both my neurosurgeon and my neuropsychologist said that it would be better if

I didn't return to my medical practice after the surgery: people were paying to see the Aimee from before, not the new Aimee 4.0. Both doctors said I was setting myself up for a lawsuit if I wrote down the wrong diagnosis or prescribed the wrong medicine. So I closed down my practice for the surgery in December of 2015 and I never returned. Because my practice was the main reason we were living in Vermont, Adam and I started talking about moving back to where he is from, in Pennsylvania, so that we would have the support of his family and friends still living there. I also realized that because the tumors were recurrent, they were never going away. Brain tumors were, and are, my life.

My attitude was very different with this surgery. No longer was it coming from a God who wanted to reign terror down upon me, and instead, I was walking through this with Him, enjoying His embrace through another difficult time. He knew what I was going through, because He had created me for this time and took on my suffering while hanging on the cross. We would get through this together, me and the Higher Power who is in control of it all. Even when things seem to get worse with our earthly eyes, it is important to trust that everything is going to be all right in the end.

I also came to see that we are all suffering. It may look different for you than it does for me, but suffering is present in all of our lives. It brings us to a place of vulnerability that can either bring us closer to God or cause us to push Him away. The Divine is continually reaching out to each of us in love, hoping that we will use our free will to choose on our own to turn and reach back. When you stop fighting and grasp His hand, you will bask in His unconditional love. God carries you when you don't have the strength to walk. Sometimes the suffering is so intense, the outside world cannot comprehend how joy can be found there. However, if you continue to seek the silence within, the suffering you are undergoing will make way for supernatural peace, hope, and joy.

In the midst of my life's struggles, for instance, I have experienced blessings too. All the things I was mad at God for were actually His gifts to me. How lucky I am to have a loving husband and three beautiful children. I completed medical school and became a Naturopathic Doctor. We were able to spend several years in beautiful Vermont, where we had an amazing home, I had a successful medical practice, we were embraced by a wonderful church, and I made lifelong friends. All of this was God's way of showing me that His hand has been guiding each step.

Those who know even a little bit of my story often ask, with genuine care and concern, if I am ok. It tends to go like this: they offer comfort by gently touching my arm, then pause to take an anxious breath, collect their thoughts, and then, with worry on their faces, ask me, "Are you ok?" Then there is always a look of shock in their eyes when I smile brightly and tell them, in all honesty, that I am good. I know that even though my body is failing me, even though my brain is ageing at twice the natural speed, even though the words don't flow and I have probably forgotten my questioner's name, I AM STILL GOOD.

This well-meaning and kindly neighbor who cares enough to ask about my health cannot always make sense of my simple response. I could say more, I know. I could tell them how often my chemo treatments are and what my prognosis is. I could talk about how I can no longer drive myself to serve at the food bank or to Mass or to my children's sports games or to get groceries. I could tell them about how hard it is to remember who has practice when and what doctor's appointment is coming up. I could tell them about all the deficits I feel from the radiation or how Adam and I have weighed all the options for treatment. But I don't.

Instead, the answer that I do give reflects the joy of knowing where I am going, and the quiet ease of letting go of all the things I am holding onto in this life. Bit by bit, the pieces of me that I thought made up who I was are being stripped away, and I see now that I am becoming my authentic self in Christ.

To the people around me, it doesn't always make sense that I can still experience joy, hope, or faith in God. My answer is simple; when you trust that God is walking every step with you, everything truly is ok. Even when my body fails me, everything is ok. For you, even when your job is no longer there or your spouse is talking about divorce or when you can't get out of bed because of depression – if you're walking each step with God, then everything will be ok in the end.

I am reminded of what Pope Francis said in his Apostolic Exhortation during the 2018 solemnity of St. Joseph. He told us then that "Jesus assures us 'You will be sorrowful, but your sorrow will turn into joy... I will see you again and your hearts will rejoice, and no one will take your joy from you' (John 16:20, 22). Hard times may come, when the cross casts its shadow, yet nothing can destroy the supernatural joy that 'adapts and changes, but always endures, even as a flicker of light born of our personal certainty that, when everything is said and done, we are infinitely loved.' That joy brings deep security, serene hope and a spiritual fulfilment that the world cannot understand or appreciate."

Even though I now have a fifth tumor and I've been in chemotherapy for the past year, I still have joy. When they see me, people comment on how I'm always smiling. My joy is in the fact that God is always with me, in the good times and the bad, not how my physical body is. When you leave late for a meeting and every light is green, it's God saying, "I'm gonna get you there on time!" Good things aren't coincidences: they are the Great Spirit taking care of you, every day, all the time.

Most of the people I talk with say they're praying for me, or offering me good wishes, or lifting me up to the universe. But then there are those who pray over me (not with me – there's a big difference) to be physically healed. Then, if I say anything otherwise, they claim that I don't trust in God's healing powers. This is quite inaccurate – believe me, if God were to physically heal me, you would not find a more grateful person! But this might not be what God has in mind for me, and it's hard to explain that to this kind of person – the reality that what they're asking for might not be granted, and that this is still ok. It's usually easier not to argue with them. So while I respectfully say "Thank you," I crack up inside because I believe the only time that any of us are truly healed is when we die. And if I'm right, then they are really just asking God to take me home sooner!

However, when I pray, it's different. I believe that solitude is not being lonely, but about being alone with God. Silence isn't not speaking, but it is listening to God. The only thing I ask for is to be open to what the Source has planned for me each day. To be "awake" to what's around me and how to best respond. That's it.

My body is getting worse daily, and yet, when I wake up, I am all the more grateful; I am all the more ok. I don't live in the brokenness of being a victim, but in the freedom of being spiritually healed. I know where I am going, which brings me joy in the here and now. On my last day, when I take my last breath, when I don't wake up, I will be better than ok. I'll be amazing! When I get to heaven, I will experience complete healing, something none of us can find here on earth. I will be my truest self when my eyes are opened to bask in the beauty of my Creator.

I know that I am not what I have done, or what I do, or what I will do tomorrow. I am a repentant and Beloved child of God, and that is enough. I am Aimee, the Beloved child of God – the God who has shown me His way through this life, and the One I hope to meet on the other side.

I have experienced pain and anguish that He did not want for me, but even this has its place. As the Bible says in Matthew 5:45, "The sun comes up for the bad and the good, the rain falls on the just and the unjust."

As Father Peter has told me, we are broken people living in a broken world. Because having free will is so important to God, He allows us to make our own choices, both about Him and about the world we live in. From our fallible human decisions, our world has come to suffer so many issues; racism and pollution and human trafficking and global warming and disease and mental health conditions and unemployment and addiction and divorce, and on and on and on... And, unfortunately, all these things cause us to suffer in turn.

But in no way does the existence of these things mean that God *wants* us to suffer. Instead, he wants everlasting life, love, beauty, perfection, and truth.

He wants you, His Beloved.

The spiritual leader Padre Pio said this: "Do not fear adversities because they place the soul at the foot of the Cross, and the Cross places it at the gates of Heaven, where it will find He who triumphed over death and will introduce it to eternal life."

God does not want us to pay the price for the broken world we live in. However, it is through our suffering that He burnishes us in His love. I have seen others suffer, and I have yearned to soothe that suffering. I have also suffered myself, and I have yearned for the suffering to stop. But on this day, today, I have made the choice to let the suffering take me. I will not try to make it stop because I am confident that God has a redemptive plan for my suffering. I choose to live the rest of my days on earth, whatever that number may be, as His Beloved until I am in His presence.

I hope you choose that too.

I sit here
watching the autumn
leaves
blowing in the wind,
bright orange and yellow
as they fall to my feet.
Seeing them disintegrate
as I walk
reminds me of the
disintegration
of my brain;
day by day
a little more.
Reminds me that
in death
there is also
life.
I am united
with the leaves,
all part of the same
cosmos.
We are sisters,
both reflecting
our brief time on
Earth;
a short chapter
in the book

of our existence.

(40 years old)

CHAPTER NINE

Reflections on Why I Went to Medical School

"Beloved, you are faithful in all you do for the brothers, especially for the strangers; they have testified to your love before the church."
3 John 5-6

    The summer between my sophomore and junior years of high school, I spent a month serving the people of Haiti. I spent a lot of my time at the mission's clinic, and this is where I met Doctor Daniel, who was trained in the capital city of Port-au-Prince.

In the town where I was serving, people would walk from faraway villages, often for several days, to wait in line at the free clinic. I remember seeing so many children waiting with their moms, all giving me heart-warming Haitian smiles despite the terrible poverty and malnutrition that was their norm.

Dr. Daniel let me assist with several procedures. I helped him insert Implanon for birth control in the arms of many women who came through, even when that wasn't the main reason for their visit. We also helped so many children. One time, for instance, we cleaned out a horribly infected, pus-filled wound on a little boy's leg, which had come from a simple mosquito bite. Dr. Daniel said this is unfortunately common. We also saw a case of lymphatic filariasis, more commonly known as elephantiasis, which is another disease that comes from an infected mosquito bite. We also gave antibiotics for opportunistic infections, anti-malarial medications, as well as Tylenol to a man with dengue fever. Another time we saw an emergency case of a young boy with cholera, who immediately required antibiotics and oral rehydration to replace lost electrolytes.

All of these diseases are rarely seen in the States, but they are very common in Haiti. I relished my time working with Dr. Daniel, and I began to see myself coming back to Haiti to provide medical care myself to people who desperately needed it.

Over one of the weekends I was there, a lady had given

birth to a deformed baby. According to the Voodoo priest, the baby must be cast out of the house in order to protect the family from evil spirits. When news of this got back to the mission, I went with another missionary to help the mother realize what she was doing. When we got there, we found the baby outside. His vertebrae had formed in the opposite direction, so his stomach was higher than his head and feet. When I carefully held him, I could only imagine what that would feel like. We finally talked his mother into caring for him and found out the next day that he did not live through the night. I was grateful that his mother spent those final moments with her son rather than leaving him in the yard to die alone. I still remember how moved I felt to be involved in this emotional situation, one of many that lay ahead for me.

Haiti was not the only place where I experienced such life-changing moments, though. My senior year of high school I got class credit for shadowing a local physician's assistant (PA). I loved how he seemed to really know each patient he encountered and also how he spent more time listening to his patients than I had ever experienced with a doctor. This PA was able to diagnose and help patients the same as the physician, who was available for him to consult with if needed. This was perfect for me, I thought. I could become a PA, which at the time was a four-year bachelor's degree, and then get back to Haiti sooner.

Because I was so impressed with this PA's skills and

bedside manner, I sent in a single application to Gannon University, the same school he had attended. Then I went to visit Gannon for a tour and an interview, right before leaving for my Discipleship Training School (DTS) in Texas. I figured that if I got accepted, then this would be God's way of letting me know I should go to Gannon. If I didn't get accepted, then I was planning on returning to Guatemala to continue serving the people there.

I remember we were staying at a mission in Guatemala City when I called home and got the news that I was the last person on a waitlist of 50. Basically this meant that 35 people were accepted into the program, and when one of them didn't attend, there were 49 people ahead of me that would be offered the spot. If the next person offered it turned down the spot, it would be open to the next person in line, and so on down the waitlist of 50 people that ended with me. With a waitlist that long, it didn't sound encouraging that I would actually get in, so I started making plans to return to Guatemala long term.

While I was driving home with Heather, my DTS friend, we stopped for the night at one of my friend's dorms at Vanderbilt. I called home to let them know we had arrived in Nashville safely, and my parents excitedly told me that an envelope had arrived from Gannon. I was pretty sure it was a rejection letter, so I had them open it and read it to me. But this is what I actually got to hear over the phone:

"Dear Aimee,

Congratulations! The Admissions Committee has selected you to become a member of the Fall 1998 entering class. Based on your strong academic credentials, you have been officially accepted into the Physician's Assistant program.

You were in the third group of students to be offered a space in the Physician's Assistant program. We are only able to accommodate 35 students in this program; therefore, to reserve your space, please submit your enrollment deposit as soon as possible."

Wait, what?? You're telling me that 49 other people didn't want the spot? I wondered aloud. If this wasn't a sign from the universe, then I didn't know what could be! I excitedly told my friends what had happened, and as soon as I got home, started preparing to go to Gannon University that fall.

Although I started school excited with my studies, by my junior year I had become disillusioned with the PA field. All of the professors for my PA classes were also practicing, and I got to hear them complaining about treating more and more patients, thus earning more money for the doctors they worked for, and all the while the doctors were doing less and less themselves. This was also right after HIPAA went into effect, and the PAs who taught in my program were all worried about getting sued by patients for tens of thousands of dollars if they didn't follow the law exactly to the letter. I was discouraged that I would graduate with a degree in a profession I feared I would not like as much as I had thought I would. So during my senior year I changed my major to science, graduating with an emphasis on healthcare.

I stayed in Erie, Pennsylvania, for two years while waiting for Adam to graduate, and during this time I got a job as an assistant in a nearby hospital lab. One of my friends at the time was looking into going to medical school, so when things in the lab were quiet, I was on the computer looking at medical schools for her. This was how I found out about the schools offering a Doctorate of Naturopathic Medicine, which interested me immediately. I learned that this kind of degree emphasized principles such as *first do no harm, the healing power of nature, treat the whole person,* and *doctor as teacher* – all things that I felt were important to patient care. Naturopathic Physicians spend a lot of time getting to know their patient so they can treat the cause of the disease rather than just treating the symptoms the disease causes. I thought this sounded really interesting, and I decided to apply to Southwest College of Naturopathic Medicine (SCNM) in Tempe, Arizona, where the weather was much warmer than it was in Erie.

My visit to SCNM was eye-opening. As the applicants sat around a table, eating lunch with a practicing Naturopathic Doctor (ND) and several students, the ND asked us how long we had wanted to be doctors. One person said that they had seen a Naturopathic Physician as a child, another said that she went to undergrad for nutrition and then found out about this program. When it came around to me, I had to admit that I never planned on being a doctor. I then explained about Dr. Daniel in Haiti, my negative experience in the PA program, and finding this school while looking for med schools for a friend. They must have liked what they heard at lunch and in my interview, because I was accepted to the spring class of 2004!

I had completed all of the prerequisite classes as part of my PA program. After changing my major senior year, I had taken almost all of the recommended classes too, such as Botany, Biochemistry, Geology, and Environmental Science. The only class I still needed was Organic Chemistry, which I was able to take at a local Arizona community college when we moved there just weeks after my first brain surgery.

Before I started medical school, I had my follow-up brain MRI as ordered by my Erie neurosurgeon. This was the scan that revealed half of the tumor was still present, which meant that I would require a second surgery. So I had to defer my acceptance for six months in order to have the surgery and then recover from the language deficits it left me with.

I was able to enter SCNM with the fall of 2004 class and soon spent pretty much all of my free time studying. Adam loved the beauty and adventure that Arizona had to offer and enjoyed living a kind of bachelor life again as well. He became good friends with a guy in my class, and they would do stuff together most weekends. This guy would show up to class without a laptop or notebook, listen to the lectures from the front row, and retain everything the professor said. I'm pretty sure he didn't take a single note during the whole time he was there! We constantly had exams in one class or another, and while I was at home studying away, he would be out climbing or hiking with Adam. The worst part was that he usually ended up getting a better grade than me, despite not studying or note-taking. Ugh, it drove me crazy!

There were times, too, when I saw reflections of my own life in my classes. For instance, we were in microbiology class when our professor was teaching us about the different kinds of meningitis. He said that there was still no cure for patients with pneumococcal meningitis, and this was ten years after my little sister Candi had died from the illness. However, he also said that they had developed a vaccine that prevents the bacteria from entering the brain, helping slow down the number of patients who present with this disease.

I was almost finished with my final year when I went in

for another follow-up MRI. This scan showed a recurrent tumor that had grown back into the cavity where they had taken the first tumor out; this new tumor had also metastasized, or spread, into some of the structures below that were closer to the movement area of my brain. Dr. Kris Smith, my neurosurgeon, told me: "I think this is definitely a more aggressive tumor and we need to get it out immediately." So I took a leave of absence from SCNM for craniotomy #3. The tumor had become a grade 3 aggressive cancer with combined astrocytoma and oligodendrocytoma cells. Now, looking back, I kind of wish I had finished my six months of school, graduated, and taken my board exams before going into that surgery. Hindsight is 20/20, as they say.

Unfortunately, I don't remember much of graduation, due to the radiation treatment I was receiving at the time. Definitely not what I imagined my medical school graduation day to be like. I do recall receiving an insightful graduation letter from my own pediatrician, who considers practicing medicine to be a sacred art.

> "Candi in her cheerful way served as a beacon of light, that planted a seed within you that has now come to fruition as you prepare to receive your Doctorate in Naturopathic Medicine. As a healer, you have the unique opportunity to bring joy when someone is made whole again, comfort

when that goal is not achievable and peace through concern and compassion. As you are now about to assume these responsibilities, I know that you will be very successful. I wish you much happiness and satisfaction in what I am sure will be a very rewarding and gratifying career for you. Much Love, Dr. Glasgow."

While taking the next three months to study for my board exams, I had to find new pathways to access the information that should have been second nature to me at that point. I figured if I passed, that would be a sign that I was able to perform the medicine I had been training for. When I got the results in the mail a month later, I was literally jumping up and down with both excitement and accomplishment. And, because I passed, this reassured me that I could safely practice the medicine I loved.

Many of my patients said that they appreciated how I treated them as I would like to be treated. Being a cancer patient myself, I knew how much I valued the time my doctors spent with me; plus, being a big sister to someone who had passed away had made me even more aware how valuable our time on earth is.

And yet, even though I got married, had kids, and started a medical practice of my own, I never lost sight of my dream to someday provide medical care to the Haitian people. Happily, in October of 2013, I got to return to the country I loved to provide healthcare alongside a team of PAs and nurses from a hospital in New Hampshire. It was amazing to return and have so much more to offer than I'd had the last time I was there at age 15. I was able to offer a listening ear, give prescription medicines and supplements to people who came in droves to every clinic we offered. I even got to pull a few teeth! I finally felt that my journey with Haiti as a very powerful motivator had come to fruition, and I was truly grateful for the opportunity to serve the people of this beautiful country as a Naturopathic Physician, something I had only dreamed of in my youth.

THE PURSUIT

Your pursuit of me
Your longing for a relationship
Unending
I spent wasted years running
Into the arms of other lovers
Trying to fill the void
Yet I would always turn back to see
Your loving gaze
Penetrating
Your outstretched arms
Reaching
To embrace me
Exhausted, I fall to the ground,
Too weak to run away anymore
Too dirty, broken, wretched
To be taken back by You
Yet You lift me
Into Your arms
Hold me close to Your chest
And comfort me,
Healing my pain, my ugly scars
Taking them on Yourself
So I can be whole again
Now I long for You alone
To know You more intimately

To be pleasing in Your sight
May my whole life
Be a praise song of gratitude
And a declaration
Of Your love and Your grace

(18 years old)

CHAPTER TEN

Reflections on Becoming a Mother

"Therefore, my Beloved brothers [and sisters], be firm, steadfast, always fully devoted to the work of the Lord, knowing that in the Lord your labor is not in vain."
1 Corinthians 15:58

Before we had kids, life was quieter, more organized, and far simpler. Making the decision to change our lives in such a drastic way took a great deal of reflection, prayer, and importation decision-making, too.

When I started medical school in fall of 2004, I thought that I would have to choose between being a successful

Naturopathic Doctor (ND) or a successful mother, but I didn't believe I could master both. I knew that at our wedding Adam and I had promised to accept children and raise them in the Catholic faith, but at the time I was more focused on being a great ND and all the financial rewards that would bring. There were also several medical students in my class who would bring their children (or "offspring" as I would snidely refer to them) to school and expect the rest of us to watch them. I remember being very unhappy with this kind of decision on their parts, thinking: *I didn't come to medical school to babysit your offspring, that's something* you *need to figure out!*

Adam wasn't ready for this kind of major change either. He'd discovered that, as soon as you drive out of Phoenix in any direction, Arizona offers beautiful mountains with great adventures. Our condo in Mesa had a tiny loft on the third floor above our bedroom where we put my "office." While I was up there constantly studying, Adam was enjoying the bachelor life with his new buddies. They would go rock climbing, bouldering, backpacking, or come over to our place to play Diplomacy or Risk on our porch, along with smoking cigars, drinking beer, and generally being ridiculous. So Adam always looked forward to whatever adventure they had planned for the coming weekend, and he was not fully ready to take on the additional responsibilities that would come with having a child either.

At the time, we used Natural Family Planning to know when I was fertile and when I was not. Something else we also had to consider was that because my life would likely be shortened by brain cancer, at some point Adam would have to raise our children alone. This played a major role in our decision making at that point.

Given all of this, the big question for us became: would we continue to avoid the days on which I could conceive, or would we choose to welcome children into our family, knowing everything that we knew?

In 2005 I started to seriously consider having a baby; however, Adam would always protest whenever I brought up the subject. "I don't really want to give up my life of doing what I want and going out when I want," he'd argue. So I assumed it was a closed issue, and it was – until December 2006, when Adam's sister had a baby girl. He went home to Pennsylvania to congratulate his sister and her husband, as well as to meet his first niece. He came back practically bouncing with excitement.

"She's so adorable!" he would crow. "She just fell asleep in my arms. It felt so amazing to hold her that I didn't want to give her back! I think I'm ready to have a baby of our own." Somehow meeting his niece had flipped a switch in his mind, and one cycle later I was pregnant.

It was funny to my classmates that I, the one who had called everyone else's children "offspring," was now pregnant myself. Adam and I came up with a funny adaptation of my previously backhanded remark about my classmates' kids: Knoffpring. Sofia was K1, followed by Everest as K2 (which is also the second highest mountain on earth) and Carter as K3. Everyone at school found it quite amusing as well. In fact, this is how Adam and I, as well as their grandparents and med school friends, still refer to my kids when texting about them today!

As soon as we found out our baby was a girl, we already knew what to name her. Years before we were even married, Adam and I discovered that we both really liked the name "Sophia," meaning *wisdom* in Greek. However, we preferred the Italian spelling: "Sofia." I also wanted to pay tribute to my younger sister, but I felt uncomfortable with using her first name. However, Candi's middle name was Faye, and that sounded wonderful with the first name we'd already chosen: our daughter's name would be Sofia Faye, or "Wise Fairy." Adam and I both liked how that sounded, and we also liked how the *f* in Sofia and the *f* in Faye sounded with the *f*'s of our last name, Knauff.

From the time we knew what our baby girl's name would be, I could not wait to meet her!

There was just one problem. When I was a kid, people always spelled my name "Amy" because that's just what they expected it to be. Back then, there were no bike license plates or keychains with the spelling "Aimee." I was determined not to change the spelling of my daughter's name to save her from the hardship I had to endure growing up. Apparently everyone else in 2007 thought Sophia was a good name too; we found out later that it ranked first in popularity! So in the end I did exactly the same thing as my parents had. Now when Sofia introduces herself to people, she emphatically adds "Sofia with an *F*" just to avoid any confusion. I do feel sorry about this but at the same time not sorry. Fifi, I love your name just the way it is!

During my first pregnancy, Adam was the best partner I could have asked for. He supported me in every way – whether it was food cravings, mood swings, or sleeping with a body pillow between us, he took it all in stride. He even said that I was more beautiful while pregnant. He's a catch, I know! There was only one obstacle: we had NO idea how to care for a baby. I know I was in medical school, but they don't have a class to teach you that! All the newborn clothes were so tiny, leading to further concerns about caring for someone so small.

"What if I drop her or roll over on her? What if my milk doesn't come in?" I found myself asking these questions and more. So many questions, so little time! When you hear someone is pregnant, you think they have all the time in the world, but when it's you, labor day comes before you know it.

I was 38 weeks, 2 days pregnant when my water broke on its own in the early morning hours of September 10th. We chose to go to the same hospital where I had had my brain surgery. I was also planning on having a natural birth, knowing that one medical intervention usually leads to others. We arrived there a little before 6 in the morning, and the nurse discovered that my blood pressure was dangerously high at 150/103. She also noted my tremendously swollen legs. My obstetrician diagnosed me with preeclampsia, for which the best cure is to have the baby. They also started me on intravenous magnesium sulfate to prevent seizures, but the problem here is that this treatment is also used to stop contractions in patients experiencing preterm labor.

After waiting two hours with no contractions because of the magnesium IV, they also started me on pitocin, a synthetic oxytocin, to give the contractions a kick start. As I watched them increase the dose from 4 to 8 to 10, I also noticed my contractions getting closer together and more painful. My nurse kept offering pain meds or an epidural, which I vehemently refused. When she checked me at 11:30, I had only dilated from 3 centimeters at arrival to 5 centimeters a few hours later. The nurse predicted that my labor would last for several more painful hours, and I was already tired. So this time when she asked me if I was sure I didn't want an epidural, I reluctantly agreed.

The anesthesiologist came out of nowhere and had me sit bent over the rolling table, my excruciating contractions still coming one after another. When I looked up at Adam, he could see I was in tremendous pain. The anesthesiologist put in a small practice dose when all of a sudden I felt the urge to push. The nurse didn't believe me until she checked and saw that it was true. It seemed that being in that uncomfortable position was exactly what I had needed to contract fully and be ready to go. She called my obstetrician around noon, and then removed the bottom of my bed and started getting the room ready for delivery. She had me breathe through the need to push until my obstetrician got there; he barely had time to get his gown and gloves on before I could not wait any longer.

As far as the epidural goes, I felt everything as Sofia came down the birth canal, including the episiotomy and the "ring of fire" as her head passed through my pelvic bone on its way out. I pushed on the next contraction at 12:32 and Sofia was finally born, after nine hours of labor. When they dried her off and handed her to me, I couldn't believe how much I loved her already.

"We did this!" I said to Adam excitedly, feeling overwhelmed with emotion. "You and I made a person together!" And it was only then, after Sofia was out, that I felt the anesthesia numbing my waist and upper legs. So much for the epidural!

They kept me on the magnesium IV for 24 hours after Sofia was born, making it hard for me to care for her. I felt light-headed and had a hard time focusing my eyes. Adam was the one to change her first meconium diapers, introduce her to visiting friends, and snuggle her first. As soon as he held her, Adam developed an instant bond that continues to this day. Sofia has him wrapped around her little finger, and she knows it! I remembered how my dad also held me first, and he used to tell me that all of a sudden his heart opened up with love. To this day, he still calls me "the apple of his eye," and when Sofia was born, I finally understood why. Sofia continues to have a very strong relationship with Adam today. She's 13 now and says no to many guys that pursue her because, "They're not like Papa." I'm happy she has set her standards so high!

When I was released from the hospital, it felt a bit unreal that we had come in as two and were leaving as three. Sofia was so small, at 5 lbs 8 oz, that Adam could hold her in just one of his arms. She also had rolls and rolls of skin that looked like she needed to be inflated to fill. The newborn clothes that we had thought were so small, now swam on her tiny frame.

I have to admit, the first few weeks were rough – Sofia would cry and cry all afternoon. I ran through the checklist but with no success: diaper, nope; hungry, nope; tried to burp her, nope. She would just keep crying until finally passing out every afternoon from exhaustion. I finally took a video of her and sent it to my online "September mommies" friend group. Several of them had already given birth or had an older child, and they all said that her cry sounded like she was tired. They asked me how often she napped during the day, to which I sheepishly replied,

"Not until she passes out in the afternoon." Like I said, just because I was in medical school did not mean that I knew how to care for a baby! My mommy friends told me that she should nap between 4 and 5 times a day. Oops! Once Sofia and I got into a routine, then, life got much easier. She slept through the night at 3 months, and had a curious, outgoing personality.

I feel like the word that I would use to describe Sofia, even from the beginning, is "honest." She is the one I go to if I ever want an honest opinion about what I'm wearing or the right pair of matching shoes. She always says it like it is – something that takes a little getting used to if you are a people-pleaser like me. However, her friends also know Sofia will always be sincere and truthful, both valued qualities in a good friend.

She was such a breeze after those first few weeks that Adam and I thought: we've got this baby thing down! We considered trying again, and by the time Sofia was 9 months old, we had another baby on the way. Adam and I were so excited! Yes, I was still in med school, and yes, I now think we were crazy too!

At the time, I had just finished an obstetrics class taught by Dr. S, an ND midwife, who had been delivering babies since before Adam and I were born. She encouraged her patients to give birth at home if there were no problems with the pregnancy. I got the positive pregnancy test right after we took our final in her class. When I called to see if she would take me on as a patient, she exclaimed, "That was quick!" and agreed to see us.

We were so excited when we found out our second baby was a boy. At the time we were planning on just having two, so one of each was perfect! I was also only the second student ever to have not one, but two, babies during medical school at SCNM. Now looking back, it sounds unimaginable, but when you just put one foot in front of the other, anything can be accomplished!

Adam and I wanted to name our second child something natural, from the earth. I remember looking at rivers around the world, but Nile or Yangtze just didn't sound right. After learning his due date was in March, Adam wanted to name him Vernal Equa Knauff, the Knauff version of "Vernal (Spring) Equinox." I immediately put the kibosh on that and fired him from coming up with any more names! When I started looking at the names of mountains, I found that Mount Everest, the one with the tallest summit, was the first on the list. "Everest Adam," I liked how that sounded. When I asked Adam what he thought, he liked it too. Mighty, strong, breath-taking, makes an impression: all words that still describe my first son perfectly!

My pregnancy with him was very different than it had been with Sofia. Everest was a very active baby! With him, my placenta also attached to the front of my uterus instead of on the inside where it would protect my organs like it had with Sofia, so I felt every single move he made. There were even times I would beg him to stop kicking because I felt like my guts were bruised. The good news was that I always knew he was there!

At my 38-week appointment, my doctor said I was not ready yet and was pretty sure I'd be back for my 39th week check-up. That Saturday night, the night before Everest was born, I was sitting a foot away from the table whining for the billionth time that I was too uncomfortable to study for my upcoming midterm exams. Everest was my biggest baby, and my growing belly showed it – if I stood sideways, I took up the entire doorway! At 38 weeks and 5 days, I was so done being pregnant and really wanted him to make his arrival. The waiting part is so hard!

In my obstetrics class, we had learned about a "Labor Balm" that was said to induce labor: 2 ounces of castor oil mixed with 2 ounces of orange juice. I also knew from studying botanicals that castor oil is a very strong laxative. It actually induces labor by causing such severe abdominal cramps that the uterus begins to contract as well. After thinking about it, I decided that I really, truly was done being pregnant and willing to try anything. To be honest, I wasn't expecting it to work, but if it did, then great!

So there I was at 9:15 pm, standing over the kitchen sink with a straw in the labor balm, which Adam had to keep stirring to keep it mixed. It was so nasty! However, every time I attempted to bail, he would remind me that I would have to study for midterms if I didn't go into labor. *Oh yeah, midterms...* I thought. *Ok, just do it!* I put the straw as far back in my throat as I could, closed my eyes, and chugged. After chasing it with a bit more orange juice, I looked at him with a bit of excitement. Tonight could be the night! I wasn't sure how soon it would work, so I went to bed and hoped for the best.

I woke at 11:15 pm with horrible cramps, and if I could have run, then I would have. As it was, though, I was forced to waddle to the bathroom as fast as I could for the worst round of diarrhea that I have ever experienced to this day. The cramps were so intense at one point that I had to grab the trash can to vomit in while still having diarrhea. It was bad. Really, REALLY bad. When Adam came in to check on me, I told him that I thought I had made a huge mistake. What if this lasted all night and didn't do anything?

Around 1 am the cramps finally went away and the diarrhea stopped. I waddled back to bed, only to wake again at 3:45 am to go pee. I noticed a nasty cramp-like feeling while I was sitting on the toilet, and I was starting to really regret drinking the castor oil because I felt so drained that I didn't know if I could handle labor if it actually happened now. Then the cramp stopped. *That was weird*, I thought.

I went back to bed and had another cramp just a few minutes later, and then a third within ten minutes. My back was also starting to hurt with each one. I wondered, *Could this really be it?* I then woke up Adam and he started timing the contractions. They were lasting an average of 30 seconds every two to three minutes. They stayed consistent but were also getting increasingly painful. Now I was sure that they were contractions. So at 5:30 am, we called the Dr. S to come, as well as Nina, my "apupunture" friend as Sofia would say, to assist. I was kind of amazed that the castor oil had really worked!

By the time Sofia woke up around 7 am, I needed to groan during the contractions because they were so painful. This time I knew what labor was like, though, so I tried my best to work with the contractions – to breathe in and down, mentally encouraging everything to open up for the baby to make his way through. Things were progressing quickly, and I knew that fighting the pain would only make it last longer. Nina walked Sofia over to my neighbor's condo so that Adam could stay with me. He was the only person who existed during the contractions, knowing exactly how to support me. In those moments his presence was everything to me.

The nice thing with this labor is that my body produced natural oxytocin instead of depending on the synthetic pitocin that I had been given at the hospital during Sofia's birth. The oxytocin provided fairly pain-free breaks about two minutes long in between each contraction. I could rest up and even talk comfortably until the next contraction began; then my focus would shift back to the task at hand.

At 8:45, Dr. S checked me and found I was at 8 cm

with a bulging bag of amniotic fluid that was causing the tremendous pressure I felt. Fifteen minutes later, I started feeling a small urge to push, and after ending a few contractions with a good push, I felt the great relief of my water breaking. It also gave the midwife and Nina quite a shower... I'm so sorry, ladies! Then I felt his head "right there" and a much stronger desire to push.

Dr. S knew from Everest's slightly decreased heart rate that he had the umbilical cord wrapped around his neck and she began hurrying to get him delivered so that this wouldn't cause complications. As soon as his head passed through, she immediately noticed that he actually had the cord wrapped around his neck twice. She reached inside to pull the first wrap over his head, and then after four more minutes of pushing, Everest was born right into Adam's arms. It was 9:15 am on the Ides of March, after only 5 hours of labor.

Adam handed Everest to me, and a feeling of complete joy passed over me. *Oh my!* I remember thinking. *I have a son!* He was quite blue at first and didn't cry right away. I remember asking if he was ok after Dr. S took him from me and aspirated his mouth and nose. When he finally cried, we all let out a sigh of relief.

While the ND midwife did a newborn exam on my beautiful new baby boy, I just lay there and watched in amazement. All the pain and struggle were immediately erased from my memory. After having Sofia, my first thought had been: "I'm never doing this again!" However, in the moments following Everest's home birth, I found myself thinking, "There's going to be one more baby, and this third child will be the one who ties the family together." A crazy intuition that must have come from Above...

Adam got to hold Everest and bond with his new son while they were rocking together in the kid's room, something he would not be able to do if we were at the hospital. What an amazing gift to be at home! I actually felt that Everest's home birth put at ease my feelings of disappointment that I didn't even know were there over some of the decisions made at Sofia's hospital birth. Being in my own home with everyone there supporting me rather than constantly reminding me that they could help with drugs I didn't want, provided a sense of peace with Everest's arrival. That moment also allowed me to find peace with Sofia's birth as well.

I have to say, though, that Everest was not an easy baby. Every three hours he needed to feed. It didn't matter how much or how often I fed him, every three hours he wanted more milk. I started to feel like he was literally eating me alive because there was no way I could consume enough calories to maintain my body and nurse him; he always wanted more. The interesting thing is that this was how I had felt when I was pregnant with him as well – he had always wanted me to know he was there. I was starting to see that with each pregnancy, I could already tell who my children were; how they made me feel on the inside was exactly who they were on the outside as well.

Everest was 8 months old when my third tumor showed up. I had to stop breastfeeding him because of the stroke and the radiation therapy I was receiving, and I think deep down he sensed that. To this day, Everest is very sensitive to everything that is happening around him. He recently asked me why I was so "pro-God," as he put it, when God was the reason for my brain tumor. As I explained that God is for life, and that human's brokenness is what causes illness and suffering, I could see the wheels turning in his head as he tried to understand. Everest is always there: crying with me when things are hard and laughing with me when things are good. I think his sensitive side is a great help to his friends too, and I look forward to seeing what profession he chooses that will enable him to continue sharing this gift with the world.

At the time we thought that Sofia, at 18 months old, was so big and grown up. Now when we look back at pictures, though, we can see that she was still just a baby herself! She was amazed with Everest at first. However, once she realized he was a permanent addition to the family, she was not interested in sharing her parents with this new person who seemed to be getting all our attention. We learned to make a conscious effort to spend "Sofia time" while Everest was napping, which helped her adjust to having a little brother around. But still! With twice the diapers to change, twice the feeding schedules to manage, and everything else that having two babies requires – all the while dealing with medical school, board exams, brain surgery, and Adam being unemployed – we had our hands very, very full indeed!

It took three years for Adam and I to decide on having a third child. After I graduated med school and passed my boards, we moved to Vermont where I worked as an intern at a local clinic during our first year there. Things in Vermont were much calmer than they had been in Arizona, and when we chose to try again for a baby, I was pregnant a couple of cycles later.

My pregnancy with Carter was more similar to Sofia's. He sat high like Sofia had, and his movements were much gentler than Everest's had been, so I just assumed I was having another girl. When we went to the 20-week ultrasound, the obstetrician asked, "Do you want to know the sex?" To which we replied, "Yes, of course!" After a few minutes of searching, he pointed out the baby's penis, to which my then 4-year-old Sofia actually burst into tears!

"Noooo," she wailed. "I want a sister!"

The doctor was quite surprised, saying that he had never had someone so young respond to an ultrasound so strongly. As a physician, though, I've always thought it was best to teach my kids the anatomical names for body parts, thus resulting in Sofia's frank response to the news.

We had no trouble picking out our third child's middle

name. Father George had been our friend since our Gannon days, present in our lives every time we really needed spiritual advice. We immediately knew that he would be our child's namesake. When I asked him if this was all right, he started tearing up and said that no one had ever named their child after him. For us, though, there was no other name that we wanted! It took us longer to figure out what this third child's first name should be, though. When we came across Carter, meaning "One who transports goods by wagon," we thought it would go perfect with George, which means "Farmer." And this is how CG, Carter's preferred nickname, came to be.

Carter always tells people he was born on the toilet, which isn't exactly true: let me explain. He did not come as early as his two older siblings. My 38th week came and went, and then my 39th week passed and still nothing. By my 40th week, I wondered if he was going to stay in there forever! However, knowing that this would be my last pregnancy, I tried to take in as much of it as I could, even at the end. Feeling another human being move around inside you is a unique experience that I knew would soon be just a memory. At the same time, though, the end of pregnancy is exhausting – especially with two other young ones running around!

At 40 weeks 2 days, Carter finally decided to make his appearance. Adam's mom had come to help us move into our new house and take care of the older two kids. This was the only 4th of July that I missed the fireworks because I was just too uncomfortable to go out. The next day I started having contractions in the morning and Carter was born 7 hours later that afternoon.

After timing my contractions for a few hours, we called our Vermont midwife. She checked me and I was only 4 centimeters dilated. My contractions were far enough apart that she said I was still in early labor. "I'm gonna go home. Adam, give me a call as soon as all Aimee can think about is birth," our midwife told us. I thought that was strange but we agreed.

Adam's mom put the kids down for a nap, while Adam gently helped me into our finished basement and turned on the TV. We only got a few stations, so we ended up watching a PBS show about how salmon go upstream to spawn. Exciting, I know. There was a point that I switched from being half-interested in the show to 20 minutes later thinking, "I don't know what this guy's talking about. Stupid fish! All I can think about is having this baby." So it looks like our midwife was right after all! She lived 40 minutes away, so when Adam called her, it would be a while until she returned.

We had planned on having Carter in my bedroom, which was two floors away – a big deal when you have to stop every two or three steps for another painful contraction.

Somehow, though, Adam and his mom finally got me into the bedroom. My mother-in-law, or "mother-in-love" as she says, stayed with me while Adam went down the hill to our garage to get something. She didn't like to see me in so much pain, but she didn't know what to do either. I was leaning over the end of our bed rocking side to side and groaning, and the only thing she could think of was to offer me some Gatorade. I impatiently replied, "I don't want stupid Gatorade! I want to have this baby!" I now feel embarrassed by my rudeness. Sorry, D! A couple of minutes later, I sensed that my water was going to break. We had nothing set up in the bedroom yet, but I knew that I could get her to help me to the bathroom by telling her I had to poop. We hustled into the bathroom, and as soon as I sat down on the toilet, whoosh! My water broke, allowing a few seconds of relief. My mother-in-law went to the window and yelled, "Adam, you need to get up here! She's having the baby!"

I remember feeling the need to push, and Adam standing there, shaking his head no, repeating over and over, "I really don't want to birth this baby!" Finally the midwife rushed in, swiftly pulling on her gloves before pushing me to the floor on my hands and knees. The midwife then realized that Carter had the umbilical cord wrapped around his neck and said, "We really need to have this baby!"

I was one of her first clients at her own practice, so that's probably why she did something that I remembered from my obstetrics class you shouldn't do: she reached inside, grabbed the crown of his head and pulled, even when I wasn't having a contraction. Let me tell you, that was very uncomfortable! After a few contractions, though, Carter's head was delivered and then with one more contraction, his body was out as well.

There was no cry, and he was really blue. The midwife took him and aspirated his nose and mouth before turning him over and gently patting his back. Adam, my mother-in-law, and I were all worried for what I'm sure was minutes but felt like hours.

"What's the matter with him?" I kept asking the midwife. Because she was so focused on the newborn, I don't think she heard me, but the lack of an answer was quite scary. My son finally cried out, relieving all of us, but he stayed blue for a while after his birth. I don't like looking at the first couple of pictures taken right after Carter's birth because they look like funeral pictures. After a while he pinked up and became more perky, but it was still pretty intense. Even thinking about it now makes me shudder, because Carter's birth was almost exactly the same as Everest's, although you'd never guess it if you met the two of them today. They're full of energy!

After Carter and I were both settled in my bed, both of my older two children came bounding into my room, so excited to meet their baby brother. I can't imagine what it must have been like starting your nap being a family of four and then waking up to being a family of five!

My midwife encouraged mothers to stay in bed with their newborn babies for two weeks after the birth. She said that spending that initial time with just the two of you forms a strong bond between mother and baby. When she told me this, I responded: "That's really difficult for me. I'm a physician with scheduled patients. It's near impossible for me to take two weeks off from work." We finally settled on one week, meaning my family would have to bring me food, and visiting friends would have to come upstairs to my room when they visited. I laid next to Carter, nursing him and snuggling him while he slept. Looking back, I now agree with the midwife; staying with your baby allows you just to be in that moment with them, which I think helps shape the person they become.

Carter is pretty much an exact copy of Adam, so much so it's crazy. The whole time I have known Adam, he has always said, "I'm the funniest person I know. My jokes are hilarious." To which I would silently think, *Only to yourself!* Even now when Adam cracks a weird dad joke, Sofia, Everest, and I often have no idea what he's talking about – and then there's Carter, laughing hysterically. You see, he also thinks Adam's the funniest guy in the world, which makes him a perfect little buddy. They also have similar body movements, similar gestures. Spending time with Carter is as easy as it is with Adam; he just gets me.

He also has a very kind spirit. Carter is loved by just about every person who meets him. Even from a young age, he could have adult conversations with someone and then remember what they said and ask about the same topic months later when we ran into them again. He would ask if their mother was doing better or their son had come home from the army yet. Carter truly cares about each person he meets, and he carves a special place in his heart for each one.

In November of 2015, as I've mentioned before, my MRI showed a fourth tumor starting to appear. The lesion was dark on MRI contrast, meaning it had not grown blood supply yet. I felt really hesitant to go through another surgery, after all I had gone through with my third surgery. Plus, this tumor had moved to the frontal lobe, which is the area of the brain that makes you, you. So I lay in bed depressed for days, not knowing what to do. Carter saw that I was upset, so eventually he climbed into bed and lay down next to me. The words he spoke next were straight from God: "Mama, it's going to be ok. I love you, so it's all ok." Relief poured over my anxious mind.

I then went to see Father Peter for counseling. I told him how I was scared my kids wouldn't know me or I wouldn't know them when I come back from this surgery; I was also terrified that I might die in surgery, and I was scared that they wouldn't know how much I loved them if this did happen.

When I voiced these concerns, Father Peter told me: "Trust that what you're doing is what God wants. I know how much you love your children. I see it every Sunday when your family comes to Mass. I see it when you bring them to the Catechesis of the Good Shepherd atrium every week. It is clear you love your kids. Now imagine how much more God loves them, and know that He will *always* love them. You have been given the gift of being in their lives for as long as He wants you to be. There may be some rough road ahead, but He's always with them. It's going to be okay."

After both Father Peter and Carter had told me that everything was going to be okay, I finally started to believe it. I feel like from that point on, I realized that it is an honor to be in my children's lives – to help them on their journey towards becoming the adults they're meant to be. Although it is a challenge at times, Adam and I are trying our best to raise three very different children to become their best selves. We choose not to hold them back in life or make them do things the way we think they should. Whenever they have new ideas or *aha!* moments, this excites us for where that will lead because the whole world is open to them. I know my parents said the same thing to me, but at the time I didn't understand. Now, though, I realize that it is a gift and an honor to be involved in even a part of my children's journeys, and I look forward to seeing what their futures hold.

It is all about spending time with the people you love. For all of us, being a good spouse, parent, or friend means that spending time together is the most valued gift you can ever give. Don't just drop your kids at sports practice – stay, watch, see what they are learning, and talk with them about it after. More than ever in this time of pandemic, we have been given the gift of more time with the people we love. In my opinion, what we need the most right now is to invest in others and have them invest in us. Reach out to people, maybe by making the time to share a video call cup of coffee with a friend or loved one you can't visit. Take advantage of this time by investing it in deeply listening to what your loved ones are saying.

While I was in the Dominican Republic last fall on a service trip with Adam and Sofia, I noticed that Dominicans are very focused on things along these lines: spending time together. Most have full-time jobs, but when you entered their very humble homes, you immediately knew that they wanted to spend time with you in their space. They value time spent sitting and chatting over a cup of café, often playing a round or two of dominoes together too. Dominicans love each other in a way that I had not seen or experienced before. After we had been there for just a week, they had claimed us as their own children.

It is amazing the capacity the human heart has to love; it just multiplies, never divides. I feel like it is so hard for Americans to experience this kind of love over the piles of stuff that we accumulate, or are working to get, plus our individualistic approach to life rather than a community-oriented one like so many other parts of the world value. In the US, all of these things often prevent us from truly seeing the greatness in each other.

Sofia recently had her 13th birthday, meaning that it's also Adam's and my anniversary of becoming parents. It's hard for me to believe that I've been a mom for thirteen years! How quickly it happened. Time is passing so fast, causing me to stop and live in the now, always appreciating each moment as it passes.

This is especially important and relevant now because the cancer is slowly taking me, and my family knows this too. For me, I try to be present each moment because I don't know how many more I've got. Encouraging conversations, both chatting about everyday stuff and deeper talks about what the future will look like, are essential ways in which I can show Adam and the kids how much I love them. For you, even if you're struggling with something that is not life and death, it is equally important to live in the present moment because it is the only moment that we know for sure we've got!

My life is just a stroke of God's paintbrush. Who you are today is the result of who you were yesterday and every day before that. For me personally, I am proud to be who I am, what I am, and how I am. I am appreciative that I was born with Beloved as my name. I also know that my husband and each of my kids were all born at this exact time in history, to be on this journey with me. They each have their own personality and their own gifts that only they can share with the world. Adam and I often tell our children how much we love and value them, but even more than that, we share with them that they are God's Beloved too. What they choose to do in life should be something they are passionate about, which will be an expression of the gifts that Divine Providence has given them. My advice to them, and to all of you, is to continue just being you and doing what you love, while you watch in amazement all the opportunities that life will present you.

Due to this pandemic, we're all facing new challenges. For you, maybe your kids are cyber-learning from home, maybe you've lost your job, maybe you live in a nursing home, or maybe you're watching the news nonstop as you try to figure out what tomorrow will bring. Regardless of the details in your situation, I hope that some of what I have learned and realized can help.

This book first started as letters I wrote to my children for major life events: graduating high school and college, things to look for in a spouse and getting married, how to care for a newborn, how meditation can benefit their entire lives. Those letters contain lessons I wish I had known in my youth but had to learn over a lifetime. Likewise, I hope this book will be a way for me to always be present in my children's lives, even after my physical body is gone. I also hope this book will help them, and you, live the meaningful, abundant, extraordinary life that the Divine intends for each of us.

I also think it would be a precious gift for your children and grandchildren if you too write down the lessons you want to leave behind. Making it a book is optional!

Little child of mine,
You will always be
My Baby
The day you arrived
Pierced
Into my fading
Memory.

Little child of mine,
You will always be
My Child
Running free and innocent
Not seeing me
As dying
But as your Mama.

Little child of mine
You will always be
My Teenager
Who has my heart
Even when I'm
Embarrassing
Around your friends.

Little child of mine
You will always be
My Young Adult

Even when the days
Get dark
And you think
No one cares.

Little child of mine
I will always be
Your Mother
Even when I'm
Gone
We can still meet
In the silence.

(40 years old)

CHAPTER ELEVEN

Reflections on My Insignificant-Self vs My Beloved-Self

"Put on then, as God's chosen ones, holy and Beloved, heartfelt compassion, kindness, humility, gentleness, and patience"
Colossians 3:12

The journey that it has taken me to realize that I am not insignificant has been long and hard. I have learned over and over that I am the meaning of my name, *Beloved*, each time with deeper understanding. For much of my life, I have felt small, inconsequential, insignificant. I grew up feeling this insignificance in many different ways, causing me to believe over and over that this is who I was.

I am very short: 4'11' to be exact. Because of this, I spent many years feeling insignificant, worrying that no one would want to hear what I have to say. In grade school, the kids would call me "speed bump" and many other insulting nicknames because of my height. I have always been on the low end of the height curve. In fact, when I was a baby they had to draw a line under the curve to graph my height! My parents and my pediatrician all thought that I would continue to grow past the 6th grade. "Maybe it will happen in college," Dr. Glasgow would say. When I didn't grow, though, I was left feeling even shorter than my actual height.

Both my parents also made me feel insignificant in different ways. When I saw the blank look in my mom's eyes while I was telling her an important story, it made me feel like she wasn't really listening and that what I had to say didn't matter to her. So, around the age of 13, I started to seek out the opinions of my friends instead of feeling like I could depend on my mom. It has taken well into adulthood for me to express how I felt to her and forgive her for that early behavior.

I also now have a very talkative 13-year-old daughter, so I can see firsthand how challenging it can be to listen to every word! However, I try to listen when my kids are talking, making an effort to really hear what they are saying. I hope that throughout our lifetimes, my children will always know they can trust me with anything, and also that they will consider my opinion along with what their friends are saying.

My dad also made me feel insignificant, but in a very different way from my mom. His opinion was always the right one, and we would "discuss" whatever it was loudly until I finally said I agreed with him, even when deep down I didn't. When I would live out of my true beliefs, he would be all the more offended because he felt lied to and this led to more struggle. I wonder if it happened this way to prepare me for my middle son, who has some of the same tendencies as my dad. By helping Everest learn how to communicate more effectively, I have also begun to understand my dad in a new way. Looking back from the vantage point of my own adulthood, I see now that I would have responded better if he had talked *with* me rather than yelled *at* me. But I also see that he loves me and was trying, in the best way he knew how, to share his morals and values with me.

Not that it always came across this way in my youth. For instance, Dad would comment on my weight, saying that I should keep from getting too fat, because no man would want to marry a fat girl. He once said this to me at our cabin in front of my friends, and from then on, I wore Umbros over my bathing suit. When I look back at pictures of myself at age 12 or 13, you can see the muscles in my legs as I kicked the soccer ball or dove into the water. I was not fat at all, and in fact, I would give anything to look like that again today! But because of what the word "fat" caused me to feel, and what "skinny" made Adam feel during his own childhood, we do not use these words in our home today.

My dad would also say that girls with scars on their face will have a harder time getting married. This was based on his experience in a college internship at an ER where someone was running with scissors, fell, and stabbed them into their face. Looking back, my dad's belief is kind of funny to me now, considering that I am happily married to Adam despite having not one, but several, scars on my head. For me, though, these scars have become trophies showing the battles we have fought and survived, not something to be embarrassed of at all. In fact, I wear them proudly!

I think we are often hurt more deeply by the people who know us the best. Learning the need to forgive not only helps me in my marriage, but it is also a valuable gift to give to my parents. After having children of my own, I now realize they don't come with instruction manuals! You do the best you can and pray that they'll forgive you for the times you stumbled. I can now see that my parents did the best job they could, and what is left are often my teenage projections of that time.

After my sophomore year of college, I applied to be a part of the Leadership and Discipleship in the Wilderness (LDW) program, where we would spend 40 days in the

Wind River Range of Wyoming overlooking the Teton Range. When I was accepted, I knew that it was what God wanted for me; the only problem was that I had never done anything like this before. After hearing about encounters with grizzly bears and using crampons for ice climbing and glaciers with deep crevasses and climbing Downs Mountain at 13,355 ft, I truly worried that I would not make it back. I literally said "Goodbye, it was nice knowing ya!" to all my friends before setting off.

At the beginning of our first hike, my pack weighed 80 pounds while I was only 120. Today everything is lightweight, but back then the gear was so heavy that I cried but put on my glacier sunglasses so no one would see it. A few days in, we got to a huge cliff that our leaders planned for us to rock climb. At the time I didn't know anything about rock climbing, and I was terrified!

Before we started the climb, our group split up to think about what name we call ourselves when we are leaning on our own strength and what is the name God calls us by. I knew right away the name God calls me: Beloved. I then remembered all the times I felt Insignificant throughout my life, and I wrote that down in my journal as well.

When we started to climb, one at a time, the rest of us on the ground called out the encouraging God-given name of the climber. When it was my turn, I took such strength from hearing the others call me *Beloved*, that I was able to climb that wall with little difficulty. I was Beloved to the group, and I saw each of them as their God-given name as well. After that experience, we all decided to use only these names for the rest of our journey together. It was very powerful! Even now, all these years later, I love getting letters from my friends still using their God-given names: Hepzibah, Content, Secure, Patient, and more.

This experience still has its applications today, too. Many people think that God made my brain tumor appear, or else that God is punishing me for things in my past. After taking Father Pete's words to heart, though, I don't believe that at all. Our God is a God of life, of love, and of goodness. So instead, I truly believe that the reason I have a brain tumor is because we have not been responsible with our collective decisions about the earth and the lives that He gave us. We didn't take care of each other or the land like we should have. We have become broken people, and from our brokenness we now have diseases like Covid-19, cancer, diabetes, heart attacks, Alzheimer's, Parkinson's, eating disorders, malaria, West Nile, Ebola, and so on. We now face the effects of global warming: wildfires, tornadoes, hurricanes, floods, and drought. We struggle with issues such as divorce, racism, gender inequality, human trafficking, and more. None of these come from God; instead, they are the result of broken people in a broken world making broken decisions.

I also believe that God has both a perfect plan and a permissive one for us. I was really moved by Father Mike

Schmitz's *Ascension Presents* YouTube video titled "Why Does God Let Bad Things Happen?" In this video, Father Mike explains that when bad things happen, they are not part of God's perfect plan. Instead, His perfect plan is when He directly wills something full of goodness and life, beauty and peace. However, when God created us as human beings, He willingly gave up some of His power by giving us free will. When bad things happen, they are not part of His perfect will, but He allows them to happen – this is His permissive will. God does not desire evil things to happen in our lives. However, He allows our suffering because He knows that maintaining our free will is for the greater good. He also knows that through our most difficult suffering, He will bring about an even more extraordinary redemption to the world. He can take something that is broken and make it whole again. Or, as Father Mike puts it: "God does not will evil, but when evil happens, it does not thwart God's plan, and that should bring us hope."

What this meant for me is that I woke up on my 30th birthday and realized that who I am was enough. Before that, even when starting medical school, I still felt insignificant and worried that no one would listen to what I knew as a doctor when they saw how short I was. On the morning of my 30th birthday, though, I decided: "That's trash! I can't change my height, so if that's a big deal for someone, I don't want them around anyways! I am who I am because that's how God made me." This forever changed how I saw myself and gave me the confidence I needed to become a stronger person and a better Naturopathic Doctor.

The search for a Higher Power and the search for ourselves are really the same journey. That's where I am with my brain tumor, and also the reason why I get up every day and say *thank you* for every breath. It's why I smile and say hello to people I pass. It is why I can respond, "I'm great!" every time someone asks me how I am. Ultimate love changes us in ultimate ways. I am confident that I am loved beyond words and completely taken care of – that I am here for as long as He wants me to be, and that when I go home, then I will be truly healed.

God's pursuit is constant. His love is unconditional and extravagant. He is always right beside us, even when we think we are walking away from Him. When you have apologized for something you've done, holding onto the guilt is like saying: "Jesus, I don't believe you died for the price of this sin." I think the Divine is only interested in what we choose to do next. We can choose to go deeper into our negative behavior, or we can choose to change and live differently from here on out. This is God's permissive will at work.

I went on a pilgrimage to the Holy Land a few summers ago. We spent each day walking through the life of Jesus, from Bethlehem to Nazareth and then Capernaum to Jerusalem. On the first day we visited Ein Karem, the birthplace of St. John the Baptist, it was also the Catholic

Feast of the Nativity of St. John the Baptist. The priest leading our group said that John was named for his calling: in Hebrew, John means "God is gracious." We celebrate his nativity the day after the summer solstice because just as the days get shorter, John the Baptist prepared the way for Jesus. As he said in John 3:30, "He must increase, while I must decrease."

That evening we went to an English Mass (others we went to were said in different languages) where the celebrating priest said nearly the same thing in his homily, except he also added that, for many of us, our call is what our name means as well. Something clicked in me, hearing this. Not only am I Christ's Beloved, but also my calling was to live out Christ's love for everyone I encounter. This changed everything! I actually found that priest the next day and thanked him for his message, telling him how much it meant to me.

Some people think that life is more like concentric circles than a straight line, and that we keep coming back to the issues God wants us to understand deeper and grow further in. I like this view because it expresses how many times I encounter the same thing only to grasp it anew with a deeper meaning each time. I am humbled at how many times the Bible addresses me personally as the Beloved. When I see or hear "Beloved," I hear Him saying, "Aimee, listen to this!" My Beloved-self keeps coming back for me to encounter in new and profound ways. I know that I am the Beloved child of God, and that I was created to shine out His love to others. I also now see that each one of us is His Beloved.

Let that sink in for a second... You are God's Beloved.

There are still days when I live in my insignificant-self instead of my Beloved-self. When I feel insignificant, I am judgmental, impatient, selfish, mean, and difficult to be around. On the other hand, when I live in my Beloved-self, I am kind, compassionate, caring, and joyful. The Holy Spirit flows through me to bless others. To this day, I continue to work on living as my Beloved-self, which comes naturally by experiencing God in both the big things and the small. I do this by knowing Him deeper through both verbal and silent prayer, meditation, going to daily Mass, and serving the poor in our community and our world as He commanded us to do. I am also able to see His hand at work in my life, every step of the way, and know that I can trust Him with everything. The most amazing gift for me is to see His face. What a gift passing over will be!

While I have the cross of brain cancer, I also know that everyone has a cross to bear. Everyone is struggling in their own way. It was from my struggle that I was able to see not only that God is continually reaching out to hold me, but also that He desires to lovingly hold each of us in this way. It has taken me almost 40 years to reach this understanding, and I am excited for what I will continue to learn each time my life encounters this lesson in the future.

We are a beautiful people, waiting to be realized by ourselves.

For each of you, my wish is that you too will truly see God reaching out for you, deeply hear what He is saying to you, and truly know how Beloved you are.

SHELL

you talk to me
but the words
whirl
in circles around my head.
only a shell of sanity remains
i cannot hear
      cannot think
      cannot care
about what you're saying.

all i want to be is me
but that is not good enough
for you.
too many problems
      too many convictions
      too scary
for you.
i feel like i'm going
crazy
losing my mind –
      or maybe i already have?

how i long to be
set free
from these oppressive burdens

that push my real self
further and further
      down
till i no longer remember
      what normal even is.
i have long since been forgotten
and only a shell of sanity
remains.

(19 years old)

empty
arms
spread wide
waiting,
reaching,
aching.

i run,
stumbling,
faltering,
in my
pursuit
of love,
of home.

You
remain,
unwavering
in patience
and love,
longing
to celebrate
my return.

(20 years old)

CHAPTER TWELVE

Reflections on Where I am Now

*"Those who were not my people I will call 'my people,'
and her who was not Beloved I will call her 'Beloved.'
And in the very place where it was said to them,
'You are not my people,' there they shall be called
children of the living God."*
Romans 9:25b-26

In my final chapter, I would like to share where I am now, because I'm sure many of you are wondering. After brain surgery #4, the neurosurgeon suggested that I close my practice in Vermont to avoid opening myself up for lawsuits if I made a mistake, since I was not the same Aimee that I was before the surgery. Adam and I prayed that God would reveal what was next for us, and we finally made the decision to move to Pennsylvania where his parents and his sister's family are, as well as many of his friends. Although it was very difficult for me to leave both my work and the wonderful friends I made in Vermont, I knew that moving was in the best interests of my family.

Even with the backstory of where I've been – physically, spiritually, and emotionally alike – I wouldn't change a thing because this has been what makes me who I am today. Sometimes I imagine how different our life together would have been if we didn't have brain cancer to deal with. When we found out about the diagnosis, just before our wedding, Adam and I decided to dive in together. At times I thought it was more than we could handle, and yet God knew better. Not only did we handle it together, but also we handled it with God at the center. Together we created three beautiful children, whom I try to be deeply present for each day. Time with my children, my husband, and other family and friends is priceless.

When covid-19 came around, quarantine was difficult for me at first. I was going to the clinic every two or three weeks for chemo infusions. My lung function had decreased because of the chemo drug I was on, and because my blood counts were unstable, I was immunocompromised. All of these factors put me at higher-than-average risk for contracting covid-19. Adam and I decided that I should be in isolation to prevent my family from exposing me, and me from exposing them. This meant staying in my bedroom while my kids were home, playing just outside my door, asking their Papa to help with homework that I knew I could have assisted them with, hearing them share dinner together without me, and playing games I wasn't a part of. I spent a lot of this time feeling very lonely for the people who were just beyond my reach.

After getting another follow-up MRI that showed the tumor was stable despite the chemo drugs I had been taking to reduce its size, I decided that I was done. No more Hand-Foot Syndrome where the medicine literally leaks out of the capillaries in your hands and feet, causing severe blisters and peeling skin, brown discoloration, and pain. No more infusions that, even as they repressed blood flow to the tumor, were also slowing my healing time and increasing my blood pressure. No more being isolated from my kids when quarantine from school was actually a gift of being able to spend more time with them. When I told my neuro-oncologist that I was done, she said we can take a break for now, but to call when I wanted their help in the future. I think she was hoping that this was not goodbye.

I continued having Zoom meetings with Father George. We have read several books by the Buddhist teacher, peacemaker, and Zen master, Thích Nhat Hanh. His work helps me understand what meditation is and what it means, what mindfulness means. Nhat Hanh ties Buddhism and Christianity together in a way that I don't think anyone else does, and I love hearing his perspective because I think he's right on. In *Going Home: Jesus and Buddha as Brothers*, Nhat Hanh writes, "The coming together of practitioners in the Buddhist and Christian traditions will bring about very wonderful things, and both traditions could learn a lot from each other. When you are rooted in your own tradition you have a much better chance of understanding another tradition. It's like a tree with roots."

"A tree with roots". . . this applies to my journey into death in a much deeper way as well. My wish is for my cremated remains to be placed in a bio-urn designed to grow a tree and plant it in the backyard. There they will be taken up into a sugar maple tree, eventually providing my family with the sap that can be turned into the Vermont maple syrup I so love. This will be the roots of who I am, long after my earthly life is finished – roots that extend deep into the ground, extending into something that will continue to serve and nourish my children, grandchildren, and beyond.

In talking about mindfulness, Thích Nhat Hanh describes it as the heart of Buddhist meditation, saying "Mindfulness is to be there, alive in the present moment, body and mind united. It is the capacity of being there in order to live deeply every moment of your daily life." In a

Facebook post from January 19, 2015 he also said, "You have an appointment with life, and that appointment is in the present moment. If you miss the present moment, you miss your appointment with life. That is very serious! Please practice mindful breathing so you can return home and encounter life."

He adds to this idea further in *Going Home*, writing that: "If you are lost in the future or in the past, you are not alive. But when the seed of mindfulness in you is touched, suddenly you become alive, body and spirit together. You are born again. Jesus is born again. The Buddha is born again."

Nhat Hanh is not the only spiritual leader who teaches this type of practice, though. Father John Main was a Benedictine monk who presented a way of contemplative Christian meditation based on parallels he saw between the spiritual practice taught by Desert Father John Cassian and the meditative practice he had been taught by the Swami Satyananda in Kuala Lumpur. Father Main taught contemplative Christians to sit still and upright for 20-30 minutes, with eyes gently closed, continually repeating a prayer-phrase or mantra. "As outside thoughts come," he taught, "simply keep returning to your prayer-phrase."

Father Lawrence Freeman, Main's successor in leading the World Community for Christian Meditation (WCCM), said this: "Meditation brings us to understand the wonder of the ordinary. We become less addicted to seeking extraordinary types of stimulation or distraction. We begin to find in the very ordinary things of daily life that this background radiation of love, the all-present power of God, is everywhere and at all times."

Both Father Main and Father Freeman recommend using the prayer-phrase *Maranatha,* which is ancient Aramaic for "Come, Lord." When I meditate, I say *Alaha,* meaning "The One" in Aramaic. This is how Jesus spoke of God, and who I believe God is, although Father George says that all of our words are inadequate to describe God. Once he told me: "We should simply say, God be's." What a powerful statement, helping us to reach beyond the limited notions we have been taught!

In Zen Buddhism, Thích Nhat Hanh changes the mantra based on what you're feeling, what's happening in your life, and where you are. As he says in *True Love: A Practice for Awakening the Heart,* "Mindfulness is not something that is only done in a meditation hall; it is also done in the kitchen, in the garden, when we are on the telephone, when we are driving a car, when we are doing the dishes."

When you are always repeating the same word or phrase in a mindful way, it becomes a part of you. It becomes like your heartbeat or your breath. Meditating allows for the person to put everything aside, and instead of talking *to* God, one can just be *with* God. His presence fills your heart and transforms your inner being. I am grateful for having the Buddhist view of Christianity and the Christian view of Buddhism. In my mind, they fit together perfectly. I think that, in every religion, Buddhist meditation has an important place.

When you turn meditation into a regular part of your life, you can both acknowledge the struggles that are present within you and also recognize that each person you encounter is suffering too. To truly love is to truly listen. When we are present in the here and now for each other, we are able to truly hear what they are actually saying, and truly feel what they are feeling. Or, as Nhat Hanh puts it: "When you become mindful, understanding, and loving, you suffer much less. You begin to feel happy, and the people around you begin to profit from your being there. . . Love is born from suffering."

Although some of us get an advanced notice that death is approaching, many of us do not. If I can offer any advice about truly being alive while truly dying, it's to be present for each other in every moment. Mindfulness will help you to become more open and more tolerant, as faith and love grow stronger within you. We all crave to be deeply heard and completely understood, and to be treated with dignity right up to our last breath.

Here's where my story takes another turn. Some would say that my condition got worse, but I see it as another opportunity to meditate – to accept what is, to love myself more deeply because of it, and in turn, to have a deeper love for those around me.

Recently, I was diagnosed with high-grade endometrial cancer. When my gynecologist called to tell me, he said that he was so sorry to have to be the one to give me this diagnosis. What he didn't know is that for years, Adam and I have joked that if I had cancer literally anywhere else, I would be ok with it. And now that I do have cancer in another part of my body that they have to remove, I'm actually grateful it will mean getting a total hysterectomy. The surgeon gets the cancer out, and I get a future with no more menstrual cycles. Sounds like a good deal for all parties!

My gynecologist was taken aback by how calm and peaceful I was with this diagnosis. I told him that I'm probably also the only patient that has been given their sixth cancer diagnosis. "Hey, as long as it isn't my brain, I'm cool with it," I said, laughing. "But even if it were my brain, I'd still be good."

He kept trying to apologize for the news, but I told him that it was my body that was growing cancer – *he* had nothing to apologize for! However, beyond the hysterectomy, I told him I am not interested in pursuing any further cancer treatment. He said that if he were in my shoes, that he would probably come to the same decision.

My next step, he said, would be to go to Gynecologic Oncology (GynOnc) to discuss surgery, and my gynecologist had a few doctors he really trusted. He was going to call after he hung up with me to see who could get me in as soon as possible. About a half an hour later, a secretary from GynOnc called to set up an appointment the following week with a very highly regarded surgeon.

I realize that what I'm going to say next might bother some of you, but I think it will also bring a smile to a lot of your faces. I have a folder both saved on my computer and an actual folder, labeled STB... meaning "Shit The Bed." When Adam and I realized that at the time of my passing, I will have STB, both literally and figuratively, we found this acronym completely hilarious. Humor does a world of good to get you through hard times! The STB folder contains my end-of-life requests, who to call upon my death, my memorial service requests, my obituary, and my acceptance letter from the Human Gift Registry to donate my body to medical school, which we'll talk about more in a bit. Adam and I both felt like it would be much easier if I made what I wanted very clear beforehand, to save him from having to make difficult decisions on my deathbed.

I brought all of my Advance Health Care Directives, as well as my Humanity Gifts Registry Donor Form, with me to my GynOnc surgical consult. I am so grateful for the surgeon who was doing the procedure. When I told her that my focus is on quality of life rather than quantity, she completely understood my decisions and was happy to sign the forms and scan them into my chart.

When I asked if removing lymph nodes could cause

swelling in my legs like you see in the arms of breast cancer patients, the surgeon said there was a 10% chance I would have lymphedema in my lower limbs if they remove the nodes. She then put in an order for a CT scan beforehand to check the size of my lymph nodes. If any were enlarged, then they would need to take them out. However, she would leave all the normal-sized nodes. The only reason to take them out would be to determine what kind of treatment that patient will have, so if I'm not doing further treatment, there's no reason to disturb them. She would also be taking out the port that was put in a year and a half ago. All of this made me feel confident that I have a surgeon who completely understands what I do and do not want. What a gift that is!

We also talked about my desire to donate my body to be used in an anatomy lab, helping teach future medical students as a cadaver. I told the surgeon that I almost feel bad when they dissect down to my pelvic area only to see that all of my reproductive organs are gone. However, when they get to my brain they're going to be very surprised! I can just see them calling all their classmates to come over and check out the brain in *their* body! I can also see myself in heaven, laughing hysterically when I hear what nickname they give my body. I hope they squish my eyeball, use the ligaments to make my hand move, and do other gross things that they hope the professor, who insists they respect the bodies, doesn't see. I expect them to treat my body with a little levity to help alleviate the dissection part of the learning process. The first day of my own anatomy lab, I sat outside crying because it all seemed so overwhelming.

When I told my new surgeon this, she smiled with me, having done similar things in her own anatomy lab, and said that she'd never thought of it that way.

When I was in medical school, one of our bodies was a 45-year-old woman who had died of breast cancer. We were so grateful that she chose to allow us to use her body as a cadaver. When we got to her breast, I remember holding the cancerous tumor in my hand, something I still picture every time someone I know gets diagnosed with breast cancer. All of the people who donated their body have given gifts to us, and I would like to return the favor and help educate the doctors of the future. Even in death, I can continue giving of myself.

It is so important to share your inner love and compassion with everyone around you, even the people you pass on the street. Smile, hold the door, be kind. Your smile could make their day and hopefully they will pass it on. There are still days when I feel insignificant. I act selfish, irritable, and am no fun to be around. However, I remember life is about serving those who are disadvantaged, whether in Haiti, Guatemala, the Dominican Republic, or in my own community. I realize that life is not about me, but about being Jesus to everyone I meet.

Meditating helps you to accept your suffering and to even be joyful in the struggle because that is the place where you can see the face of God, or the face of Buddha, within yourself. Whenever people talk to me about their suffering – trouble in their marriage, a difficult disease diagnosis, their grief for a loved one, a miscarriage, or any other struggle they are experiencing – I always direct them to lean on God through it all.

For God is always with you, even in the hard times. When you get to the end of your rope, stop and say "God, I need you." He will lovingly embrace you in His arms – arms that have been reaching out to you the whole time. You will know His incredible love for you as He carries you through the times when it's too hard for you to walk.

Knowing that I am Beloved is the source of the joy, acceptance, and peace that radiates out to others. I hope you will also find peace in your suffering as you too learn to live as His Beloved.

You have created me in Your image,
    Oh Lord.
You have created me
    With emotions
    Modeled after Your own.
In the pain that life brings,
In my deepest, darkest nights,
In the endless desert I wander through,
You were always there
    To bring light into the darkness,
    Rest to my weary soul,
    Living water to quench my desperate thirst.
You never once left my side.
You were never shocked at the questions
    The doubt
    That plagued my heart and mind.
Oh Lord, acquaint me with Your suffering
    As You have made mine Your own.
Help me to clearly see
    The Intimacy I long for,
    The loving gaze of your eyes.
I will turn my face to You,
    Bask in the warmth of Your smile,
    Captivated by Your sweet voice.
To you alone will I remain true,
    Without regard to the hardship
    Life may bring.

May I know Your healing touch,
 That I may touch others with Your love.
In my suffering,
 May I experience Your joy.
Just as you were broken for me,
Let my pain bring Your heart for others.
As my love is refined in the fire,
 Let my faithfulness
 Bring glory to You.

(17 years old)

BLESSED, MERCIFUL MARY

Blessed, Merciful Mary
On my own
I am weak
And always sinful,
Even on my best day.

Therefore I ask you
Mary, Mother of Mercy,
An example of
True trust in God,
Help me be more like you.

Virgin Mary,
Who carried the
Divine Face of Mercy
Within you,
Intercede on my behalf.

Mary, Queen of Heaven,
Help me to also
Know His love for me,
Embrace His plan for me,
And say yes like you.

(39 years old)

Thanks for reading my memoir. Hopefully, along the way you have connected with some of the lessons that God has shared through me and will apply them to your own life's struggle.

Peace be with you, from one Beloved to another.

ACKNOWLEDGEMENTS

First of all, I want to thank my husband, Adam, for always believing in me and for being an amazing caregiver through it all. Thank you for taking this journey with me. I love you with all my heart.

Also, thanks to Mom, who has worked tirelessly to transcribe and edit my work. Thank you as well to Alissa for all your help on this book. It would not have gotten done without your encouragement!

I also want to thank Father George for our weekly book readings that have helped me see the beauty and depth in meditation. Thank you too for the encyclopedia of resources you share, for meeting me where I'm at each time we talk, and for writing the foreword for this book. You are a very dear friend.

Thanks to Meredith for the honor of using your picture on the cover. It was exactly what I was looking for, and with you being a photographer, I'm grateful that the photograph I will end up using is one of yours.

I want to thank Dad and Lesa for giving constructive feedback on this manuscript. Thanks, Rob and D, for always being there for me. Mrs. McCane, thank you for believing in me all those years ago.

Thanks to Dr. Bessie for getting my story out there, promoting my book, and getting me in touch with your daughter. I am also thankful for Angela, Maria, and the Lael Agency for all you have done.

I am also grateful for all the healthcare professionals involved in my medical care over the years. Your dedication and commitment have helped me more than you know.

Thanks to spiritual leaders such as Pope Francis, Thích Nhat Hanh, Father Mike Schmitz, Father John Main and Father Lawrence Freeman, Henri Nouwen, Saint Padre Pio, and Father Peter for the life-changing insights that your words have brought me.

Last but certainly not least, I want to thank God for speaking through me, and in doing so, sharing with others the lessons You have taught me. I am eternally grateful to be Your Beloved.

www.ingramcontent.com/pod-product-compliance
Lightning Source LLC
Chambersburg PA
CBHW071433070526
44578CB00001B/93